Freedom

Andrew McKay

BALBOA.PRESS
A DIVISION OF HAY HOUSE

Balboa Press books may be ordered through booksellers or by contacting:

Balboa Press
A Division of Hay House
1663 Liberty Drive
Bloomington, IN 47403
www.balboapress.com
1 (877) 407-4847

Print information available on the last page.

ISBN: 978-1-9822-4828-4 (sc)
ISBN: 978-1-9822-4829-1 (e)

Balboa Press rev. date: 06/03/2020

Contents

BOOK: III: Europe 1972

Prologue

FOR ME, THE word is Freedom. That is my Talisman that invokes my deepest desire. I am not referring to the kind of freedom we enjoy in the U.S., that is liberty which is a gift that makes the freedom I am talking about easier to obtain- though not a requirement. My freedom is freedom of the soul, freedom from outside sources of religion or politics and the media. It is the freedom to be who we truly are; our unique God- intended dreams and desires that emerge when our minds are quiet from those outside sources or our own numbing mind chatter. I believe there is a place within us that is a peaceful spiritual communion with our Source, without judgment or anger; a place where there is a love of life just as it is and a love of who we are, just as we are now. Of course, retaining this is an elusive quest for the hero's journey in a world that appears to be designed by man to derail that freedom.

Memories of Europe come to me like uninvited friends that are always welcome and represent a time when freedom came easier without the demands of marriage, family, career and other people's idea of success. It was in May of 1972 when I was 24, on a train from Salamanca, Spain to Lisbon, Portugal that the idea of freedom became embedded in my soul. Most of what happened is real but over the years I blended circumstances to create a fantasy that serves to remind me of the liberating lesson learned that day.

The landscape of northern Spain is strikingly similar to that in Central California, my home, as I watched it pass by while thinking of my travels for the first four weeks of a planned six month-journey. I had gone from Amsterdam to France and then Spain alone; meeting a few individuals that were characters who seasoned the journey with interest, but mostly I was left with my own thoughts that often bordered on loneliness. Suddenly the train began to slow as we approached the village of Fuentes De Onoro, the last stop before crossing the Portuguese border. I was told by the conductor, that I would need to change trains and there was an hour wait.

Stepping off the train, I took in the sight of the station that was little more than a concrete box with a couple of thick wooden doors and realized I didn't want to hang around there so I decided to explore this small town in the time I had to wait. I swung my backpack over my shoulder with my worldly belongings including a light sleeping bag, a plastic tube tent and a small guitar that I had purchased in Pamplona to relieve my loneliness.

What a sight I must have been. My hair was not as long as it would soon be but certainly longer than what was common in Spain and Portugal. The standard apparel for this trip was a plain blue T-shirt, bell bottom jeans and square toed boots with brass buckles on the sides fastened by straps sewed to the front of the boots. My thin 6-foot frame towered over most of the Latin residents and with my green backpack and Spanish gut-string guitar I definitely stood out. It was a Saturday afternoon and the weather was warm but puffs of white clouds in a brilliant blue sky intermittingly blocked the warmth of the sun.

My thoughts conflicted between enjoying walking down this little town with its ancient stucco shops and cafes that probably looked the same as it did during World War II or maybe World War I and at the same time the self-consciousness I felt being the only American and that I was as different as if I had just arrived here from Mars. I continued walking, fighting back my uneasiness while resolving to be in the moment. That was why I traveled I reminded myself; for the experience and adventure. So what if I was different? But it was a battle. It had been a battle my whole life.

At the end of the street I could see in the distance that the road seemed to stop at the entrance to a forest. As I approached, I realized the street did stop and a dirt trail carried on into the towering pines that stood before me. The smell of pine and the slightly damp humus that lay like a carpet below the trees beckoned me to walk further. The late afternoon sun was still above the trees but the height of them created shadows so it became darker and colder as I followed the trail. I had no intention of getting lost in a forest and missing my train, but before I turned around I came upon a wooden bridge that had been built over a small river from some unknown source moving noisily over the rocks. I stopped, letting the sound sooth my mind. I planned to turn back when I saw a clearing in the distance with rays of light cascading through the trees. I continued to walk across the bridge feeling like each step I took had a purpose as if some force was drawing me to the light. Without warning, the trees opened to a beautiful green meadow covered with white flowers. The trail stopped there and so did I as I stood at the edge of the meadow taking in the serenity of the pastoral scenery before me.

Then I saw her. She was midway into the meadow sitting on the grass surrounded by flowers. I began walking again with the same purpose noticing there was no one else in sight except this lady and only the sound of birds somewhere and the breeze rustling through the surrounding trees. Moving into the open area I could feel once again the warmth of the sun. As I got closer, I could see her soft wavy-blond hair falling over her shoulders. She was wearing a white dress, more like a gown that flowed over her legs as she sat on a colorful embroidered blanket. She was holding flowers and it seemed from the distance there was a radiance emanating from her whole being.

I was normally too shy to approach her, but I couldn't stop myself; it was a magnetic pull I couldn't explain so I kept moving toward her. She looked up at me as I got close and she smiled, her beautiful blue eyes twinkled with happiness.

"Sit down with me" she said in English.

I did as she asked placing my backpack on the grass surrounding the blanket. "You speak English," I questioned more as a statement.

She just smiled and handed me her flowers, yellow and white daisies. "You are American?"

"Yes".

"Why are you here?"

"My train was not leaving for an hour, so I just walked here."

"No, I mean why are you in Spain?" she asked with kind concern.

"I'm traveling because I want to see Europe. I'm drawn to this continent for some reason – I can't explain but I saved my money for a year to do this."

"Are you alone?"

"Yes".

"Are you lonely?"

"Sometimes."

"But you are free."

"Yeah, I guess I am. I hadn't thought about it."

"And freedom has a price; loneliness. Until you learn to be whole by yourself, then you will never be lonely."

"What do you mean?" I asked.

She smiled took the flowers from my hand and placed them beside me on the blanket. Then she took my hand in hers facing me and looked deep into my eyes. "I can read you and know more about you than you know yourself. You are free, temporarily, but still a prisoner of your own making. You won't allow yourself to be completely free because you are too concerned about what other people think; to be completely free you must first know who you are and follow your true heart and soul. You travel because you are running away or running toward something that will make you happy. Most people live their lives doing that. But to be free, really free you must give yourself permission to be yourself. To have confidence and joy as you approach everything in your life. You see, you will never find that happiness outside of yourself. Wherever you go, whoever you meet and are with, you will never be enough until you are completely free of your own self-imposed 'shoulds'."

Her smile became more radiant as she said, "There is so much you will learn in your life. You are young and have many years to experience and learn but the greatest lesson is learning to be whole by yourself. Your soul knows what you are to do. Trust in your soul. It is God speaking to you."

There was a slight wind now and the air was becoming cooler. I looked up at the pine trees in the distance and could see the branches swaying slightly with the wind. I looked back into her penetrating eyes but did not say anything, I didn't need to. I knew intuitively she knew what I was thinking and feeling; I had a swelling in my chest and a feeling of happiness and well-being that I rarely felt. I wanted to stay here forever just holding her hands and looking into her radiant face.

She spoke, "You are feeling the way you do at this moment because you are in touch with your own soul, the soul of your Creator, which is with you always. Nothing at this moment maters; other than being in the moment. It is the pinnacle of existence and it is yours to experience whenever you want."

She released my hands and stood indicating for me to do the same. "You need to go now to catch your train. Take what I have told you; it is a gift." She then reached with her hands and touched my face with both hands and kissed me on the lips. Her touch and kiss ran through my body like electricity, but it wasn't passion I felt but rather well-being. She whispered, "Go-be free and have a wonderful life."

I just stood there looking at her not wanting to move. "You must hurry," she said and so I did. I picked up the pack and guitar and walked briskly away toward the bridge only turning to look back before I crossed it. She was not there; the meadow was empty. I then began to run across the bridge and through the woods until I reached the street, then began walking quickly through the town toward the station. How long had I been gone? It seemed like all day. Was it only an hour?

As I approached the station, I could see the train I was to take and it was just beginning to move forward. I ran toward it removing my pack as I approached; the cars continuing to move slowly. Between two cars was an open platform and I threw the pack landing it guitar side up. Then I moved alongside the train pacing the speed which was a fast walk then simultaneously I grabbed a hand rail above the steps catching it and jumping up and on. I made it. As the train was pulling away, I turned and looked at the station several yards away now and the people looking at this crazy American kid and I smiled. The people smiled back at me as the train moved away.

At that moment I could have died a happy young man; I felt happy and strong, confident and at peace. It was a complete sense of freedom as I watched the town disappear and the landscape now moving faster past me. I continued to stand on the platform totally in the moment; the woman's voice was still in my head, "be free." I could not have felt freer than I did at that moment.

There were many adventures that awaited me that summer. I would meet friends that would be in my life for its duration. It was the adventure of a lifetime and I would not trade the experience for a million dollars. In the years that followed, Europe became my freedom and the girl in the meadow my creative symbol of desire to find the confidence to have that freedom. Who was the girl? A month after that day at the border town of Fuentes de Onoro I met her on the island Ibiza. But that is another story.

BOOK ONE

EUROPE 1969

Chapter 1

HOW DID MY quest for travel, freedom and adventure begin? I knew from my earliest memories there was something embedded deep in my soul that longed to do more or be more than just eke out a mundane existence. I was not a good student, nor was I talented in sports or really anything else. More than anything I was-and probably still-am, a dreamer. I longed to leave my hometown of Fresno and immerse myself in a larger life away from my parents. My dream destination was Newport Beach, which I had discovered over the years because my paternal grandfather lived in nearby Corona del Mar. I continued to struggle in school; attending Fresno City College after high school graduation in 1965, for no other reason than what my mother instilled in me: that college was my only hope if I wanted to do anything worthwhile with my life. The first year I nearly flunked out and was put on academic probation. Suddenly another very strong motivator for staying in school came to me: an army pre-induction physical request.

The war in Viet Nam was escalating and would eventually become a national tragedy. The weight of this and the somewhat recent assassination of President John Kennedy created disillusionment to a huge generation of Baby Boomers. It was a time when that generation, my generation, was more interested in social injustice and anti-war causes than the stock market and accumulation of wealth. As for me, I was a fringe player. I didn't believe in the war in Viet Nam, but I also did not believe in marching against the United States. The path for me, I decided, was to stay in school and so I forced myself to work harder and continue-at least for the time being my mother's dream of staying in college.

It was at the end of 1967 that I received my acceptance to Long Beach State University, no small accomplishment for someone who was branded by my high school counselor to not be college material. My good friend, Rick Thomas, and I had looked into living on campus or pledging for a fraternity, but we both decided that was not for us. Instead we found a small one-bedroom bungalow on 33rd Street a half block from the beach on the Newport

Peninsula. It was a post-World War II construction with grey wood-slat siding and heavy white window trim. The best part was that the rent was only $100 a month, $50 each. Since I had a budget of $100, I could pay half the rent and have the rest for food. We were about 30 miles from the college, which was probably irresponsible on our part, after all gas was 25 cents a gallon, but my parents gave me a gas credit card to cover that expense. The other irresponsible part of living in Newport Beach was the distraction from our studies. Still, life has a way of opening up ideas that at the time seem insignificant and I was soon to have one of those openings in my life.

Irresponsible or not, I have to admit that living near the beach was a dream come true. Even though it was winter, I loved walking to the beach, kicking my shoes off and taking in the fragrance of cool, ocean air and listening to the constant squawks of seagulls and the crashing of the surf. Ever since I can remember I always felt at home near the ocean. I did not know it then, but that peaceful comfort would include seashores wherever I traveled.

Our street on the Newport Peninsula was comprised of mostly small houses and two-story apartments designed to be rented inexpensively in the winter. Then throughout the summer properties would be rented weekly for much more money. Next door to our little bungalow was a large 3-bedroom house, easily three times the size of ours. The occupants were high school teachers at a nearby Orange County school who were also coaching football. The coolest of the three drove an orange Porsche 911 and sometimes I would see him on weekends driving away with a surfboard on his car. To me, he appeared to be the ideal of the person I would like to be.

I don't recall how I first met him. I believe Rick befriended one of the other coaches and we were invited one evening to come over and look at their house. All three of the coaches were there and after introductions, we were given a tour of the house. There were two items that immediately caught my attention: the first being an old refrigerator that sat on the back indoor porch and had been designed to hold a keg of beer with a hole in the door that allowed a spout to be on the outside. Not only did I think that was outrageously cool but even cooler was the fact that we were offed a beer even though at the time both of us were only-20-years old. The other item? It was the one that would change the course of my life. We walked into the living room with our beers in hand and I looked above the fireplace at a large black and white picture of Earnest Hemingway as he was with white hair and beard. The lines in his face and deep penetrating eyes told me here was a man who had lived a full life. Joseph Hampton who was the cool guy with the Porsche noticed me staring at this amazing portrait and asked, "Do you like the picture?"

"Yes, very much, I read his biography; he had an interesting life. Is that yours?" I said.

"It is. I'm an English teacher and teach literature."

"And he is your idol," I don't know why I said that, probably because he would have been mine.

"No, I don't idolize him but I do like his writing and he represents something that has become a passion for me."

I looked at him waiting for what that was.

He continued, "Traveling in Europe."

Suddenly I was swept away with visions of Papa Hemingway in Paris and Pamplona and asked, "Did you go to the places he went?"

And for the next 30 minutes, Joe as he was called and I talked of his travel in Europe. Finally he said, "If you ever get a chance to go, especially while you are still young, do it."

Over the rest of that school semester Joe and I became friends. We surfed together a couple of times and I got to know the man who was not only cool but kind and intelligent. In July of that year, I turned 21 and Joe took me to a private club in Santa Monica for lunch and drinks. We would remain in touch for a couple of years. He married and had a son and eventually we just stopped seeing each other. Still the vision he had set in my consciousness was the force I needed when a year later an opportunity presented itself as if the whole thing had been divinely planned. Perhaps it was.

The school year of 1968 had been a remarkable year for me as well as tragic for the nation. In April, Martin Luther King was assassinated. That June in Los Angeles Bobby Kennedy was shot and killed. These men were dynamic heroes that were taken from us much too soon. With Bobby gone it was an easy path for Richard Nixon to be voted in as the 37th President of the United States. The protests from the under-30 crowd became even louder. Rick Thomas moved to Fullerton where his parents lived and I moved to Costa Mesa with John Martin, a very good friend from Fresno. After searching for jobs most of the summer, I found one delivering papers to news stands for the *Santa Ana Register*. As the school year came into sight, John and I looked for another place near the beach and found a three bedroom on 40th street. We invited another connection we had in Fresno, Steve Alexander, who was a brother of one of John's friends and a character, whom I had met while on 33rd street, we called Big Frank, who was from Brooklyn. I went back in school for the fall semester and continued my job with the newspaper delivery.

I was very much into music as a break from school and work, playing a 12 string Gibson that my parents had given me that Christmas. The music of that time-period that I liked was Simon and Garfunkel's new album *Book Ends,* and another album by Jeff Beck, *Truth,* with a new singer named Rod Stewart. Bob Dylan, of course, continued to crank out great records including *John Wesley Harding* and *Nashville Skyline.* My movie heroes were Steve McQueen in *The Thomas Crown Affair* and Paul Newman in *Cool Hand Luke.*

Our apartment sat on the corner of 40th and Seashore just a half block from the sand. It was good to be back near the ocean after spending the summer in Costa Mesa. The structure was a downstairs flat with a very large front patio ideal for hanging out with the many friends that frequently stopped to be close to the beach and to people watch. I was the only one of our group making a serious effort to go to college; in fact all of my roommates and our friends were only part-time students, which made my effort at working and driving to Long Beach State each day even more challenging. School continued to be something I felt I had to do, but did not like very much. Still, I was determined to see it through.

In the fall of 1968, I changed newspaper delivery brands from the *Register* to the *Los Angeles Herald Examiner* with my route becoming more centered in Newport Beach and the small towns along the Coast Highway. Monday through Saturday I set my alarm for 5 a.m., drove to a pick-up location, loaded my car, a white Ford Ranchero, with several bundles of newspapers and then drove to the news racks and stores in Newport, Balboa Island and Corona del Mar. I carried *a bag of dime slugs* to open the racks and fill them with the latest edition. The delivery of each location was based on the average number of papers sold each day. At some of the better locations I would drop 7 or 8 papers, but the average was about 6 per location. I actually got pretty good at it and could open and empty the rack of day old papers with one hand while filling the rack with the new additions all in one smooth motion. It actually was a good job for me because it only took a couple of hours and I could listen to the radio in my car and enjoy the sunrise as I drove. I became acquainted with the delivery men from the *LA Times* and the *Santa Ana Register* and a few of the locals who hung out for early morning coffee and doughnuts at Dad's on Balboa Island.

In those cold, early winter mornings as 1969 became a new year I would drive over the bridge to Coral St. on the island while it was still dark. The yellow & white street lights illuminated the quaint shops and restaurants along a two block business district that was a summer tourist paradise but by contrast, quiet in the winter. The island had not changed much since I was a 7-year-old when my grandfather and I would walk along the avenue and sometimes stop at the toy store peering through the window at some treasure, like the plastic pirate ship he bought for me. That same toy store was still there. By the time I had made my stops on the island, the sun would be rising and I would stop at Dad's long enough to have a doughnut and a couple sips of coffee before I put the lid on it, finished the delivery and headed home to shower and get ready for my morning classes.

The only real glitch about the job was Sunday. The Sunday edition had to be stuffed with inserts and wrapped with comics, so I needed to wake by 3 a.m. and drive to a rented garage along Pacific Coast Highway where a delivery truck would drop about 150 morning editions to be put together. I would then spend the next couple of hours putting the papers together. It was hard enough waking so early, but I often went to bed on a Saturday Night with a party in the living room and wake Sunday Morning with the party still in progress as drunken friends made cracks about me working at 3 a.m. It was a bit unnerving and as I look back, I wonder how I could have lived in a world of responsibility of work and school in an environment of irresponsibility and reverie. As would be the case so many times, I would try to balance my life with contrasts only to remain perpetually out of balance.

One of the guys who hung out at our house was Jerry Lawhorn; he was a friend of a friend and I didn't know him very well. Jerry was one of those smart nerds that had a wicked sense of humor that made him cool enough to hang with. One afternoon he stopped by with another friend, Ed Davis. I was doing some homework on the dining room table and took a break to visit. After the usual sarcastic pleasantries, Jerry said, "hay Andy, you want to go to Europe?"

That was random, I thought but my interest was suddenly at a new level, "yeah" I said, "I would love to go to Europe, are you going?"

"I think so. My parents are in this Dutch club and they have travel specials to go to Amsterdam. I want to go but not alone. Nobody I have talked to can go and I don't want to go alone."

I figured Jerry had exhausted just about all his contacts before he would ask me. "So, if I could go you would go?"

"yeah, I want to get a new car and found out that if I bought it over there and stayed for six weeks, I don't have to pay an import tax and the savings would practically pay for the trip. Also, my sister is living in Germany and she and her husband could show us around."

Jerry still lived at home and his parents had money, he could do something like that, for me it was a doubtful possibility. Still this could be an opportunity to do what Joe Turner talked about. "What are we looking at for cost?" I said.

"The plane ticket is something like two hundred forty. The club my parents are in has amazing costs. It is a charter flight, not a regular airline."

"Great, is it going to get there?" I quipped.

"No man, it is really cool, they have gone several times."

"Ok, look, I do want to do this, but I doubt if my folks will go for it. Give me a few days and I will let you know."

After they left, I thought about what had just transpired. I really wanted to do this and realized if I had to move heaven and earth to make it happen I would do so. Only I had no idea how I was going to do it.

That is the other irony of life. If you want something bad enough and believe it will happen, there is usually a solution. I didn't have an extra dollar to spare but somehow, I knew that this was important enough to look for a way. Nervously, I called my parents to float the idea and the possibility. They had been helping me with college and I knew they would not be too enthusiastic about spending money for a summer jaunt to Europe.

My mother answered the phone as was normal since my dad hated to talk on phone after a day of work. We got through the preliminaries; I usually did not call without some agenda.

"I know this will sound crazy", I started, "but I have this friend, whose parents are in some travel club and I have been invited to travel to Europe this summer." I gave her the details of the trip.

There was dead air space for an uncomfortable few seconds…then she said, "How much is it going to cost?"

My heart was racing; this would be one of the toughest sales of my life. "The airfare is $240 round trip. It is really a bargain and a great opportunity."

She wasn't buying it, but at least she was being nice. "I'm sure you would like to take a trip like that", she said, "but we just don't have that kind of money lying around. We have made sacrifices for your education already, but I'll let you talk to your dad."

That was a relief, he was not as sweet as her, but he was more open to this kind of opportunity, although Europe was not what he would choose. She handed him the phone; "What's up", he said.

I relayed the information to him and followed with, "I really want to do this. I know you guys aren't crazy about travel to Europe, but this is a real bargain and if we could figure out how to do it, maybe I can pay you back some day". Of course, I had no idea how I would do that but I was desperate at this point.

Pause…then after another heart stopping moment; "You know, I have this life insurance policy on you that should have some cash value. I'm not sure how much but probably enough for the cost of the flight and I am sure you will need spending money. Let me check what it is tomorrow, and I will let you know. If it is ok with your mother, I'm ok."

"Really?" I practically yelled, "Thanks dad!"

As we ended the call in that phone booth on the corner of Newport Blvd. and 30th street, next door to the laundromat I had been going to for the last year, I could have danced right there. Life Insurance, I thought. What better ways to use it, than while you are still alive?

Chapter 2

SUMMER ARRIVED, THE school year was over, and I continued working that summer taking on another job at the Rueben E. Lee Restaurant as a dishwasher. The flight to Europe was not until the end of July. We were still at 40th Street, the result of a one-year lease we had negotiated the previous September. Over the course of early summer, we had continued to have many visitors many, friends from Fresno coming to enjoy the beach. I don't recall when I moved my worldly possessions, which wasn't much, back to my parent's house, but I remember watching the first Lunar Landing with the rest of the world on July 20th at their house. In addition to that amazing historical event, my sister Becky was to be married before I left for Europe, creating a hubbub of activity.

The evening of the departure, my parents insisted on taking me to LA to see me off. It was obvious, even though they could not understand my interest in going to Europe that they were very excited about my adventure. I think if he could have, my father would have told everyone he saw, "my son is going to Europe." We got to the terminal about an hour and a half before our departure time and found Jerry with his parents.

After introductions, I looked around taking in the scene; it certainly was a no-frills flight; just a plane near a hanger with everyone waiting outside in the dark as if waiting for a bus. It felt like my parents were dropping me off for camp. The group we were traveling with was a mix of experienced travelers and former citizens of Europe going home to visit. All of us were to be in Europe for six weeks but fortunately there were no group tours or itineraries. We would be able to go wherever we wanted, which is exactly what we planned to do.

The flight was delayed, waiting for some people who were late. Normally I would have been irritated but I was soaring with excitement, so I didn't care. Finally, it was time to board the plane. We said goodbye to our parents who had waited there patiently and climbed the stairs to the Boeing 707 that would take us to Amsterdam. As I turned to take a last look before entering the plane, I had no idea that my perspective toward life would never be the same again. That, I discovered was the magic of travel; the adventure of meeting people out of your normal world and the experiences that broadens your outlook toward life.

We settled in our seats, each of us on the aisle across from each other. As the plane taxied down the runway, I looked at my watch, it was almost 2 a.m. Jerry immediately fell asleep and slept nearly the whole trip, but I was too excited. I was sitting next to an older couple, Seventh Day Adventist Missionaries who had traveled all over the world. They were originally from Holland and spoke several languages. The man explained that he was in a concentration camp for four years during the war. It was hard to imagine that just 25 years before this gentleman spent four years of his life in a concentration camp. These were extremely kind people and I felt it was my good fortune to be able to talk about Europe and the war as experienced by someone who had been there. I would discover that the Dutch people were still bitter toward the Germans and there was definitely some animosity in their references to that Country. Twenty-five years later the wounds had not completely healed.

We landed at Schiphol Airport at about 8:30 in the evening. We had lost most of the day in flight, and even though I had not slept I was surging with energy because of my excitement. Here I was in another country where English was not the primary language. What I found though was that most educated Dutch citizens, speak 3 or 4 languages including English. Typical to how we would travel throughout Europe, we had no reservations, but Jerry assured me we could get a room through the KLM information counter and that is exactly what we did. We booked into the Hotel Bierenbroodspot, for no other reason than it was inexpensive, and it included a breakfast.

We were directed to a bus that would take us to the city and as it pulled away from the airport, I was struck by the yellow street lights that lined the streets casting a magical almost Disney like look. The sun had gone down and in the darkness the lights reminded me that we were in a whole different world.

The bus dropped us off at the center of town and we had no idea where our hotel was, so we got into a cab and gave the address to the driver. What a surprise as we pulled up to the "hotel". I thought the cab driver had made a mistake; we were in a residential neighborhood of brick houses. It was a very nice neighborhood but there were definitely no hotels around. We checked the address, walked up to the front door and saw a little plaque on the wall about the size of 5x7 picture-frame that said "Hotel Bierenbroodspot". How strange. Jerry rang the bell and the latch released. We entered a hall with a flight of stairs directly in front of us. An older woman stood at the top of the stairs and told us to come up. It occurred to me as we walked up the stairs that our hotel was really a residence and the owners were just renting rooms.

We were greeted by two ladies who showed us our room and then invited us to have coffee in the living room. It was a lovely old world flat, very well kept, with lots of local art, quite unlike what I was used to in California. I absorbed the sight of this beautiful little home; its warmth and the fact that here I was in Holland. I also realized that I was very comfortable in this setting. There was a knowing, that I could not describe; that I belonged here, and I was going to love Europe. Never had I taken a class in school that instilled in me the desire I had at that moment to learn. This was the real thing.

"So, I see by your passports that you are from California", the older of the two women said with a heavy accent but very good English. "We always wanted to go there, but just never have".

We talked about life in California and then I asked, "so this is your home?"

The younger woman, named Sophie explained, "yes", pointing to the older woman, "she is my mother and she and my father owned this home for many years, before the war. I grew up here and when my father passed away, we converted our home to a hotel."

Her mother, Lotte, said, "it was a way to provide income for us." She looked at her daughter, who I guessed was in her late forties and Lotte, late sixties, "we enjoy it and get to meet so many interesting people."

It was obvious they were not only proud of their home but enjoyed sharing it with travelers from all over the world. We talked for about an hour or so; they seemed to enjoy hearing about America as we discussed comparisons between our two countries. Finally, at about 11:00 they said they were going to retire for the evening. Jerry and I, who were not even close to being tired, decided to go for a walk. We walked the neighborhoods close to our hotel, obviously a well-kept middle-class section of the city. I was amazed how clean the streets were. There were more yellow streetlights which continued to create a charm right out of the movies. We crossed some canals; the stillness of the dark water below reflected the night sky creating an enchanting ambiance. I kept reminding myself that this was just the beginning.

The next morning, we woke early and had a wonderful breakfast of soft-boiled eggs perched on small stands, cold ham, cheese and lots of toast and rolls with butter and jam. Our plan was to pick up the car, leave Amsterdam and make our way to a town in southern Germany, Garmisch-Partenkirchen, which had an army base where Jerry's sister lived with her soldier husband. The new car was a 1969 Volkswagen square back station wagon that would be perfect for sleeping when we were on the road. Everything had been pre-arranged and once Jerry signed the necessary papers, we were off. We decided not to spend too much time in Amsterdam, since we would be back before flying home and we were anxious to get on the road. Jerry drove through the city, swept away by the traffic, totally lost looking for the road to Belgium our first destination. Of course, I was totally useless as a navigator, relying on a city map, but somehow, we managed to find the right direction and left city.

The Netherlands countryside is all farmland, very flat and green. Because Netherlands is a delta for five major rivers, irrigation is not a problem. Amazingly over a quarter of the country's coast is below sea level, which is why the famous dikes are so important. We drove on, passing windmills and farmhouses until we reached the Belgium boarder. As we were waiting to pass through, a dark-haired young man sporting a heavy beard, walked up to the car and in German asked a question.

I looked at him from the passenger window and asked, "Do you speak English?

"Oh yes," he replied, "I wondered if I could get a ride to Brussels."

I looked at Jerry and he nodded, "why not?" As luck would have it, he would later prove to be very useful to us.

Chapter 3

THE CITY OF Brussels is about 50 miles from the Netherlands-Belgium border. We were not overly impressed, especially after being in Amsterdam. I found the city to be old and without charm. The people we encountered were not very friendly, perhaps because we were young and looked like vagabonds. Whatever it was we didn't like it, so we decided to move on. Our new German friend, whose name was Michael wanted to go with us: he didn't like Brussels either, so the three of us drove on toward Luxembourg. Michael was 19 years old, spoke very good English and as many young Europeans did, traveled during their holidays by hitchhiking. He lived with his parents and was going to a University during the school year. Jerry and I enjoyed his company and it was a great way to get a perspective of this part of Europe from someone close to our age.

We rolled into Luxembourg at 8:00 p.m. and looked for a place to eat. In 1969 there were very few American fast food restaurants but there was a European hamburger chain called Wimpey's, named after the character in the Popeye cartoons who loved hamburgers. We walked in and tried our first European hamburger. Since I am a connoisseur of hamburgers, my favorite food, I decided to make the comparisons to the American burger. They weren't bad, the meat was a bit different but overall a good substitute. The French fries, called Pomme Frites, were good too, but most Europeans use mayonnaise on them rather than catsup. I couldn't handle that.

After dinner we walked around the city, something we would do in each city we visited; it was fun to discover the soul of the town and its people. Luxembourg was a much prettier city than Brussels, very modern in architecture at that time. We stopped into a bar to have a beer and listened to Country Music. The place reminded me of some of the bars in my hometown of Fresno, but it was dull there, I guess the locals weren't into Country Music, so we left. Our next stop was Club 31, a discotheque that was alive with young people and good rock music. The girls were beautiful, and the beer was good but expensive for our budget, so we didn't stay long. It was getting late anyway, and we had no idea where we were going to sleep that night.

We got on the highway leading out of the city and drove for a while, until we saw a pasture. Jerry pulled the car off the main road and we decided this would be a good place to sleep. Michael had a tent, so he and I slept there, and Jerry slept in the car. I drifted off thinking of those pretty girls at Club 31.

I woke the next morning to the sound of cows. I looked out of the tent and saw a whole herd practically walking over us. It was only 6:30 a.m. but it was definitely time to go. We drove most of the day, and as we were driving, I turned on the radio and began looking for a good rock station. Michael said the best station was Radio Luxembourg, which was so strong it carried over most of Europe. We dialed in and throughout the rest of the trip, we had great music with English speaking D.J.'s. From Luxembourg we drove across the top of France and finally to the German boarder where we ran into our first major hassle. The boarder guard spoke no English but what he was trying to say was our license plates were not current. Thankfully Michael was with us and was able to interpret. While all this was going on, I noticed that the river at the boarder was the Rhine. It was not what I expected, and I thought, this must have been a beautiful sight at one time, but now it flowed on concrete. Finally, Michael and Jerry got the matter resolved and we continued our drive through Germany, arriving at the town of Freiburg, where Michael left us to head east as Jerry and I continued south toward Switzerland. The terrain was quite different from the Netherlands. Beautiful mountains in the background and rolling hills of green that made the scenery picture postcard perfect.

It was about 8 pm when we arrived at the Austrian Boarder. We had covered four countries in one day because of the route we had chosen. Rather than just driving through Germany to our destination of Garmisch-Partenkirchen, we went around the western boarder to the south deciding that we would cross over the Bavarian Alps. We chose this route because on the map it looked shorter, and it was a chance to see some of the other countries. Of course, we hadn't anticipated crossing the Alps at night.

By the time we arrived in Innsbruck, we were exhausted from lack of sleep the last two nights, and the jet lag that finally caught up with us. We were still 4 hours away from Garmisch and we considered just staying the night and getting a fresh start in the morning. Of course, that would have been the sensible thing to do, but we were young and adventurous, and sensibility had no place in our world at that time. We wanted to get to Jerry's sister's and didn't want to spend money for a room or sleep in the car. The idea of a free bed was appealing enough to head over the mountains. Our experience in California of having good roads on the main highways, even in the mountains, led us to believe it would be the same here. It wasn't. The roads were bad, winding, steep and dangerous. Jerry was driving and I hoped he had the skill to manage those curves because there was nothing between us and the side that dropped hundreds of feet below. It was nearly midnight by the time we drove into the valley and could see the lights of Garmisch-Partenkirchen.

Chapter 4

FOLLOWING THE DIRECTIONS Jerry had been given, we made our way to the apartment where his sister lived with her husband. They were waiting for us. Jerry's sister Stephanie was a tall blond with somewhat sharp features and a strong presence almost like the stereotype German woman; although I don't think she was. Her husband Mac was probably her same height, which was maybe 5'10; looked athletic and handsome and had a cool about him that made him a leader in most situations, although I got the feeling, not in the marriage. With them, was a very pretty young girl, Anne, who had waited at the apartment because she wanted to meet us. I'm not sure how they knew we were coming that night, perhaps Jerry had set it up and that is another reason why we pushed forward that night. We stayed up for another couple of hours, sharing our adventures so far, and getting to know each other. Mac was in the army, stationed in Garmisch, and because he was married, was able to rent an apartment away from the base. His job was serving as a lifeguard at the near-by lake.

Garmisch-Partenkirchen is 50 miles south of Munich and lies at the base of the Zugspitze, Germany's largest mountain range at nearly 9,000 feet high. Garmisch was the sight of the 1936 Winter Olympics during Hitler's reign and now was one of Germany's premier resorts with skiing in the winter and water sports at Lake Eibsee in the summer. The US Army used part of the lake as a retreat for the military personnel and their families. What I would discover was that this was like a country club with the military as the members. Not what I had pictured the army to be. If everyone could be guaranteed duty like this, the army wouldn't need a draft. But of course, Mac and Stephanie were lucky, and they knew it. Anne was the daughter of a career military officer but was staying with friends for the summer and working at the lake. She was only 16 but looked like she was 21; tall, blond with that porcelain skin that is reserved for the young. In addition, she had a very shapely figure. But it was her personality that rounded out the attractive package. She was bubbly, self–assured and as we would discover, very playful. Jerry and I looked at each other as she talked and didn't need to say a thing; we were both enchanted.

Garmisch-Partenkirchen, which we all called just Garmisch, would become our home base in Europe. For the next few days Jerry and I got to know the many friends of Mac and Stephanie and the local hangouts that were both military and German. My experience there was mostly American because of the people we became friends with, but the German culture was not lost on me. I leaned early that it is the experiences we have in life that gives the most meaning to particular events so my memory of Garmisch is only good. The beautiful grass valleys with winding roads that dropped down to the lake; the Bavarian architecture nestled in a forest of pine trees at the base of the granite Alps rising magnificently above the timber line are memories that remain, even after so many years. But even though I have always appreciated the characteristic beauty of each part of the world, it has always been the people that interest me the most. So, as I awoke on our first morning in Garmisch, I had no idea what experiences I would encounter that would shape my memory of this wonderful place.

We all slept past 9am; it was much needed sleep for me, and it was wonderful. We washed, taking turns in the hall bathroom, dressed and headed to the American Service Center where we had breakfast. Mac drove Jerry's car as he sat in the passenger seat and I squeezed in the back with Stephanie and Anne. At the center, we met one of Mac's good friends Al, and then sat down to a typical American breakfast of bacon and eggs. After we ate, we exchanged our money for German Deutch-Marks. Since Europe in those days had different currency for each country, and since we had been in six countries in two days, we had a conglomeration of money. Keeping the different currencies straight would be a confusing process but that was just part of the experience that made it interesting as well as challenging.

Mac was not working that day, so we drove to a small local restaurant/bar called Psychobrau, appropriately named for the group we were with. Mac and Al convinced Jerry and I to try some local drinks along with the wonderful German Beer we ordered. First, we tried a shot of what was called the Hunter's Drink which tasted terrible and kicked like a horse. Then we had a shot of Steinlagger a lot like Gin, but I was told much stronger. We ordered another beer and settled into a nice party mood.

By now, Anne who was drinking along with us was, to my approval, becoming much friendlier. Europe at that time did not have the strict drinking laws that we had in California, so no one hassled her about drinking. We all decided to take a drive to the lake and since there was no more room for Al, I volunteered to sit in the back of the station wagon and Anne jumped in with me and snuggled up like I was her one and only. Ah, life was good, here I was in a great German resort, partying with the in-crowd and this gorgeous young lady had eyes only for me. But of course, it was short lived. At the lake she detached, probably since she worked there, she didn't want to be seen hanging on me, at least that's how my ego rationalized it. But later when we got back to Mac and Stephanie's apartment she began flirting with Jerry. He was happy but I realized she was just a young girl who was having fun and I was not going to bother with her. Yes, easier said than done; the reality was, my little romance with Anne was not over yet.

We were only at the apartment long enough to change our clothes then we all headed to the Grill, the favorite watering hole for the Americans and ordered more beer. Stephanie and Mac didn't stay long but for some reason Jerry and I, who were playing on still limited sleep, decided to keep going. I think it was mostly because Anne was there and neither of us wanted to surrender. We began bar hopping with Anne as our guide and I realized she knew guys all over town. She was a popular little lady. Our final act of insanity came at a place called John's Club where Anne and I ordered a John's special, which consisted of a pint glass half filled with Champaign and half bourbon. Jerry was already going down for the count, so he declined. We never finished the drinks but what we did drink, did some damage. How we ever got home I don't know. Jerry was getting sick, so I drove. The music on the radio was playing a new popular song called Je T'Aime, which was to become our theme song for Europe. With the music, Anne and the buzz from the booze, I was in a fool's paradise and loving every minute of it. I somehow managed to find my way to the apartment and we all stumbled up the stairs. Jerry was green and Sue was falling and bouncing off everything in sight and laughing at herself. Stephanie was not overly amused with us, but then who likes waking up to a bunch of drunks. We all went to bed and I slept like I was dead.

I never appreciated the benefits of being young until I got older. But really, who does? The ability to party until late, wake in the morning and be ready for another full day is a young person's game. I slept until 9:30 when Mac got us all up to go to the lake for breakfast. He was working that day and so was Anne who worked at the hotel at the lake. After breakfast Jerry went with Stephanie shopping for food and I stayed at the lake. Some of the recreational activities there included water skiing and the Army had a boat to use for that purpose. I hadn't skied much but I decided to give it a go and went around the lake a couple of times before I wiped out. I dove on the boards for a while, something I knew how to do since I was a diver in high school, then sat and talked to Mac and Al who were life guarding. What a great group of people these were. I began to have conflicting feelings, because I was anxious to travel on and see more of Europe, but I was having so much fun here, I didn't want to leave. Yet I had come to see Europe and being in Garmisch and hanging out with Americans was a lot like being home.

My grandfather used to tell me "Andy, you never are satisfied with what you are doing; if you are on the merry-go-round you want to go on the Ferris-wheel, when you're on the Ferris-wheel you want to go to the Arcades. You need to learn to enjoy what you're doing while you are doing it." That is advice I wish I had been able to embrace. Whatever I did, I always figured I needed to go to the next place. Of course, the benefit of that was, lots of experiences, but it would take me a few more years to learn to appreciate the moment, without thinking about what was next.

That evening Mac barbequed steaks in the little back yard behind the apartment. It began to rain, and we had to move the barbeque under a tree until the steaks were done. It rains a lot in Germany, but it was pleasant since it was still August, it wasn't too cold. After dinner the four of us drove to the base to see the movie "Planet of the Apes". We then stopped at the Grill had a couple of beers before going home. I recall that we were getting news of the events that led up to death of the actress Sharon Tate and later learned about Charles Manson. The horrific nature of her murder reverberated from Los Angeles to the Army Base in Garmisch and I remember where I was when we got the news.

Our original plan was to leave for Italy that morning, but Mac encouraged us to stay one more day.

"Come on you guys, one more night. There is a beer-fest in town, and you don't want to miss that." Mac said.

I was beginning to realize that our experience in Garmisch centered around drinking; not that I had a problem with it, but I was really ready to head out. Mac persisted and was a good salesman; we finally said yes.

While Mac was working that day, Jerry and I decided to see a German castle that was nearby. We drove to the Schlob Linderhoff, a small castle built by the German King Ludwig who was envious of Louis XIV of France and created his own lavish quarters. The castle is more like a palace and is similar to the palace in Versailles, France. It was all very interesting, but we soon became bored and decided that swimming at the lake would be much more fun. I do love history but at that time in my life when it came to castles and museums, a little went a long way.

Back at the lake, we heard that some of the guys were going to play baseball at the ball field the Americans had erected in town. Jerry and I decided to check it out. A game was just beginning with the Americans challenging a German Soccer team. It was a riot; the Germans knew nothing about baseball, so it wasn't even a close game. I'm sure if we had played soccer, they would have slaughtered us. The game finally ended when it got dark, so we went back to the apartment then left for the beer festival.

The German Beer Festivals are wonderful events and I was glad we had postponed our departure for a day to attend. Once we were inside the tent and seated at a long table shared by whoever happened to be there, a very busty woman with arms like a heavy weight wrestler brought our beer. The beer is served in one-liter mugs and she carried five full mugs in each hand, which just amazed me. The German beer is stronger than what we are used to in California and of course very good. We drank our first beer and then decided to walk around. Like an American fair, there are carnival games that generally, in my experience, a way to throw money away. Not so for Mac

We walked to a booth that had softball sized balls and lead shaped bottles. "Hay guys, think I can knock those bottles down?"

Jerry whispered to me that Mac had played baseball in high school and was a good athlete. "I wouldn't bet against him", he said.

To my surprise and those who watched he was deadly accurate with his throws. Within a few tries he managed to win a large doll and a teddy bear. We walked out of the festival feeling like heroes. Of course, the evening would not have been complete without a stop at the Grill for a night cap.

Chapter 5

IN THE MORNING we packed to leave for the next phase of our Adventure. After breakfast at the army diner, we stocked up on cigarettes and canned food from the commissary, gassed up and said good-bye to Mac and Stephanie. We hadn't seen Anne for a couple of days, and I was sorry I did not get to say good-bye to her but our plan was to stop back through after we had spent some time in France, Spain and Italy. There was no specific itinerary; we thought we would spend a couple of weeks in Southern Europe before going north to the Scandinavian Countries.

Driving back over the Alps was easier in the daylight and quite beautiful. The panoramic views from the height of the mountains were spectacular. We passed through Austria deciding not to stop but enjoying the scenery, then arrived at the Austrian-Italian Border around noon. After so many border crossings since we arrived in Europe, I presumed this would be just more of the same, but it became very complicated. To purchase gasoline in Italy at that time, if you bought gas coupons, it was much less expensive. But it was like buying drink tickets at a fundraiser; you just don't know how many you are going to use. If you buy too many you end up with coupons you won't use and if you don't buy enough it will be more expensive later. So, we just made a calculated guess. Then we had to buy Auto Club Insurance to cover theft because there was a lot of it in Italy. The whole process took about two hours before mercifully we were finally on our way again.

The highways, called Autostrats, were excellent but they were toll roads and by the end of the day we had spent over $10; a lot of money on our limited budget where every penny counted. Without a real destination we continued to drive the rest of the day; stopping at about 6 pm on the side of the road to have dinner; which consisted of cans of stew and hash cooked over a can of Sterno; a jelly like substance that could be lit and provide enough heat to warm the contents. After dinner we drove on to the outskirts of Venice. It was getting dark, so we decided to look for a place to sleep and stumbled onto a campground that was relatively inexpensive, the first inexpensive thing we experienced in Italy. There was a little store with a patio at the campground, so Jerry and I bought a couple of beers and sat out enjoying the pleasant Italian summer evening. How wonderful to be so free, sitting at an outdoor table talking about life as we saw it then; so young with so much to look forward too not only on this trip but in our lives. This was a terrific break from school and my world back home. I was beginning to have thoughts of not wanting to go back. I loved this life.

The next morning, we were eager to get on the road; our destination; Florence. As always, my desire was a mixture of contrasts. I loved the cities, with the bustle and activity; the people and the pace of city life is energetic and exciting. Yet the drives through the country were amazing to me. The European landscape from north to south is simply hypnotic in its perfection. Whether you are looking at the flat fields of Holland, the picturesque green hills of Switzerland and Austria or the magnificent Alps of Southern Germany, it is truly breathtaking. Italy, of course, had its own unique charm. From the north which was mostly green rolling hills to the south with golden fields of vineyards; the scenery made our drive just one more element of the experience that resonated in my soul for a lifetime.

As we drove toward Bologna that morning, another unexpected event was about to occur that would change the character of our trip. We saw a hitchhiker along the rural road we were on and stopped to give him a ride. His name was Sean and he told us he wanted a ride to Florence. Sean was tall, about 5'11", thin with a scraggly beard and uncombed mop of long, brown hair. He had a great smile and his eyes twinkled with wisdom and humor. As we talked along the way we learned that Sean was from England and had been traveling the whole summer on a very strict budget which explained his skinny physique. He was 25 had a pleasant personality and both Jerry and I immediately liked him. His plan was to spend some time in Florence and then head south to Rome.

Florence is one of those cities that inspire you. Set on the Arno River it is brim full of art; from paintings and sculptures to architecture which made sense since this was the birthplace of the Renaissance. As you walk through the streets you can see a world that is teeming with history and present-day commerce at the same time. We spent the whole day exploring museums, cathedrals and shops and realized we could stay a whole week in Florence and not see everything. My best memory of that city is walking up to Michelangelo's statue of David. It was by accident because we weren't looking for it. Located in a museum called the Galleria dell Academia, the statue stands majestically. Since I had not studied art history and didn't know much at the time about Michelangelo, I probably didn't appreciate the significance of this incredible work of art. But as I looked up at this magnificent piece of sculptor I was moved by the perfection. Many years later as I read about the life of Michelangelo the memory of David and Florence helped me appreciate this master renaissance artist.

By early evening we had enough of sightseeing and set out to find a campground for the night. In Europe there are campgrounds around every major city, and they are well marked so it wasn't too difficult to find one that had a beautiful view overlooking the Florence. The three of us rested for a while then cooked another fabulous dinner out of a can. With our restricted budget, going to some nice Italian restaurant was out of the question. It was a matter of priorities and fine dining at that time in my life was not an option. So, we celebrated our adventure in Florence with cans of Franco-American Spaghetti. The irony was not lost on us. It tasted pretty good with the real Italian bread we bought in town.

After dinner we walked to the camp store and bought a bottle of wine. For the price we paid it probably had a vintage of about a week, but we didn't know or care. Sitting at a table in the outdoor patio we discussed tomorrow. "Sean", I said, "We aren't going as far south as Rome."

"Where are you going then", he asked.

Jerry jumped in, "We want to go over to France and then Spain. Rome is too far out of the way. We are trying to see as much of the Continent as possible in the short time we have."

"How long is that?"

"Total of six weeks", I said "and we already have used up one of them."

Sean looked out at the landscape as he took a drink of wine. "Perhaps, I will not go to Rome either and stay with you Yanks, if you'll have me."

We laughed and Jerry said ok with me, how about you Andy?"

"I'm good. If you get to be a problem, we can always throw you out."

"Just so you know, mate," Sean said, "I can pay my own way, but I can't pay for gas. I just don't have the money."

Jerry said, "It's ok, that doesn't add any expense for us."

So, it was settled. Since we were not going as far south as Rome it was a change of plans that he was ok with. For Sean, even though he appeared to enjoy our company it was a matter of economics. He had been traveling for quite a while and was on an austere budget that made Jerry and I look like we were the picture of opulence. Traveling with us meant traveling in a style that he hadn't had most of the summer and it was at no extra cost to him.

We finished our wine and Sean began talking to some girls that were sitting at another table and managed to convince them to join us. Two of the girls were American and one was French, we had a party in the making so we ordered two more bottles of the cheap wine. Jerry and Sean worked their charm on the American girls, so I was left with the French girl who was somewhat pretty but spoke very little English. This was my first attempt at trying to make romance with someone who didn't understand what I was saying. It has been said that success happens when preparedness meets opportunity. I thought about the one semester of French I took in high school and how I dropped it because I was flunking out. I definitely was not prepared. I'm sure she finally got bored with my attempts to be smooth while fumbling at trying to communicate and went back to her camp site. The boys seemed to be having a better go of it than me, so I left them and went to our camp site and crawled in my sleeping bag. Feeling the effects of the wine and staring at the starry night I fell asleep.

I awoke the next morning surprisingly without a hangover. That rotgut we were drinking should have killed us. I noticed the two American girls were sleeping at our camp site, I guessed the boys lured them over but didn't get very far after that. Sean was not feeling well as he woke, and I assumed he did have a hangover. He had been living so miserly, saving money by not eating much that his health had deteriorated. He didn't have the stamina to drink like Jerry and me.

We packed up the car, said good-bye to the American girls and drove south toward Pisa. Sean was getting sicker and we had to stop the car several times for him to get out and throw up. This was no ordinary hangover; he was really hurting. When we got to Pisa Sean had no strength, he got out of the car and lay down on a park bench while Jerry and I walked around the city. We viewed the tower from outside but decided not to go in. It was much larger than I had anticipated and was quite impressive. When we came back to the car, we tried to get Sean up.

"No, leave me here", he said, "I don't want to be any trouble."

"Sean," I said, "we're not leaving you here, get in the car."

The whole scene reminded me of some B movie where the guy gets wounded and tells his companions not to bother because he will just slow them down and to go on without him. Of course, being the true American heroes that we were, we weren't going to leave him, so we drug him to the car, pulling down the back seat to make room for him to sleep. He must have been delirious with his illness because he told us later, he didn't remember any of the conversation on that bench.

We spent the rest of the day driving while Sean slept. We traveled along the Gulf of Genoa which is on the Riviera. The landscape was quite beautiful and different than the rest of Italy. Over the years I have found in my travels that the coast, any coast is like home to me. Whether the ocean or the sea it is like an old friend who is always there. The familiar cool breezes, the smells and the overall feel are soothing to my soul. We drove through town after town, Genova, Savona, and San Remo all picturesque and charming.

Of course, we weren't going to leave Italy easily; at the boarder the guards told Jerry we had used our gas coupons too fast and had to pay a fine to leave. I guess we should have stayed longer; in any event we had broken some rules. We were thinking what kind of BS is this? The problem was, we had no money left at least not in Italian Leers and besides we didn't want to give them anything even if we had. The guard looked at us, thought about it for a moment and then said, "you have two minutes to get out of the country." I don't know if that was supposed to make us feel bad, but we were leaving anyway so to us it was not a problem; arrivederci Italia.

Chapter 6

AS WE CROSSED into France it was getting late, so we found a place by the side of the road, outside of Monaco, to spend the night. Jerry and I rolled our sleeping bags on the ground and left Sean sleeping in the back. We had checked on him throughout the day to make sure he was still alive; he was breathing so we figured he would be ok; vagabond medical evaluation.

I awoke with my body aching; that ground was hard. We didn't have any French money and we were hungry. Sean was feeling better but still quite weak. We drove on to Cannes and parked the car to have a look around. This was such a famous town because of the film festival, and we wanted to get the feel of it. We found a bank open, and changed our traveler's checks to francs, then looked for an inexpensive place to eat. Walking through the narrow streets and alleys we realized this was not a town for the budget minded traveler. Of course, Cannes has its own charm with old world construction, monstrous buildings along the Promenade de la Crosette, lined with Palm Trees and running parallel to lush beaches that begged us to spend the day. But when you are 22 and have very little money it is not a place to hang out for very long. We went into a bakery and bought a loaf of wonderful, fresh baked bread and walked to the beach to have our breakfast. There it was the Mediterranean Sea. It was still early so there was not a lot of activity at the beach, but it felt good just to be there. You could take the town; the charm was wasted on us, but the beach was where I wanted to plant myself. We knew though, that if we were going to live on anything but bread and water we needed to go to Spain where we were told it was much less expensive.

We jumped on the main highway and missed the rest of the Riviera; our strategy was to get to Spain as soon as possible. We did find a small café along the way with prices much more reasonable than Cannes. We ordered steak and frittes and after a couple of days of canned food it was like going to heaven. The rest of the day was spent driving through Southern France. We finally arrived at the Spanish boarder at nine o'clock at night. We were all pretty tired at this point and getting a bit edgy, so we decided to find a hostel or some cheap bed for the night.

We discovered that there were no hotels that had rooms available and after several inquiries, we were standing outside of one hotel wondering what to do next when a man walked up and told us he had a room for us for 100 pesetas each; about $1.70. I'm not sure where we got the pesetas at that time of night, probably a change kiosk near the border. The man did not speak English, but we figured out what he was saying and followed him to an apartment complex where he showed us our room which had a shower too. It was nice to have a bed to sleep on but the whole night there was noise and I wondered if these people ever slept and the ones that wanted too, how could they. It was bustling with activity nearly all night long.

When I awoke, the first thing I did was take a shower; I needed it. Of course, there was no hot water and although I never could get used to it, I learned to expect it. The places we stayed just didn't have hot water and I began to realize how much we take for granted in the U.S. that was a luxury to many Europeans in the late 60's. Jerry and Sean woke after me and each took the opportunity to wash the road dust of several days with a cold shower. Then we packed up the car and headed out, stopping at a little café for coffee. What we got, was two ounces of strong coffee in a small glass; my first espresso. I found with a little sugar it was pretty good.

Spain at this time was still ruled by the Fascist Dictator General Franco. By 1969 the country was encouraging tourists but still had a very conservative, Catholic presence that discouraged the kind of lifestyle that we had experienced in Garmisch. This fact, however, was for the locals; tourists that came from Germany and England as well as adventurous American travelers, at least in tourist areas were free to have fun; within limits. Over the ensuing years the country let down the rigid structure but not until Franco passed in 1975 was it close to the cosmopolitan appeal of the rest of Western Europe.

Our destination was Sitges, a small seaport village outside of Barcelona. While we were in Garmisch, Mac had told us that Sitges was a great party beach town with plenty of pretty girls. It was understood that our destination spots had a lot more to do with having a good time than cultural interests. The drive took us most of the morning and afternoon. We stopped at a small restaurant along the way for lunch and I ordered Paella, a dish that is uniquely Spanish made of saffron rice and seafood or whatever the chief has available. I have since had Paella with chicken, crayfish, squid, sausage, shrimp and have often joked about what else may be in there. But regardless of the jokes, it is without question one of the great dishes of the world and on this particular day I experienced it for the first time.

We arrived in Sitges at about five in the afternoon, found a campground on the edge of the town that was walking distance to the beach. The landscape of this campground was quite different than that of Germany and the other northern areas we had visited. This campground offered mostly dirt, with very little vegetation. It reminded me of Mexico; not pretty but close to the beach, which made up for any lack of scenery as far as I was concerned. As soon as we parked into our designated camp site, we locked the car and headed for the beach and a walk around the town. Surprisingly even that late in the day there were thousands of people on what was a very small beach. One of the great lessons in life is, when you build your expectations on what other people tell you, you can often be disappointed. People will talk positively about some event or place based on their experience and your experience is totally different and you wonder, what was so great about it. If we were planning on visiting some sleepy fishing village with no expectations, we probably would have been thrilled with Sitges, but we envisioned a paradise with opulent sandy beaches and hundreds of beautiful women just for the taking. That's not what we experienced.

The scene at the shore was somewhat like the one in Cannes; with Palm Trees lining beautiful mosaic-tile walkways and a large, what appeared to be church, on a hill overlooking the lovely waters of the Mediterranean. We found a place on the beach and Sean struck up a conversation with a pretty Australian girl. Sean was the ladies-man of the group; mainly because he was the one who had enough nerve to initiate conversation. Jerry and I went for a swim in the clear blue water but found there were no waves. To me, at that time, a beach without waves was like swimming in a lake. We fooled around in the water and the beach for quite a while before deciding to go back to the campground and change into dry clothes so we could discover the night life.

As the sun began to set, which in Spain is around 9:30, the sky became darker than normal as a storm appeared to be moving in. It was very humid, and it felt and smelled like rain. We made our way to the campground patio as the lightning and heavy thunder began. This lightning was very close, too close in my opinion, but the effect was quite dramatic. Then the rain came down and for nearly an hour did not let up. There is something about this kind of weather as the sun is setting that generates an energy in your soul that, at least for me, makes you forget about your thoughts and only on the aliveness you feel. We ordered beers and said "Sitges is a bust."

Sean just stared at the storm, probably thinking that even if it was a bust, this night was pretty awesome. He said, "Let's give it another day; we still haven't seen much of the town."

The storm finally subsided but we kept drinking even though we decided this Spanish beer was not very good. My objective was to drink enough to make that hard ground bearable to sleep on since I was the one that usually slept out of the car, mainly because I did not like sleeping with someone else in that confined space.

The next day the weather was beautiful; clear and hot. We packed up and left the campground still trying to decide whether to stay or leave Sitges. Even though we hadn't been impressed so far, we were reluctant to leave for fear that we would miss something. Since it was so hot that day, we decided to find another beach and found one that actually had some surf. The surf was small, but I managed to get some bodysurfing rides. Since surfing at that time was not a popular sport in Spain, I figured it probably looked a bit strange to the Europeans.

After a while Jerry and I decided to explore the town, so we left Sean at the beach and we began walking. The streets were narrow, meandering past residences and shops. There was a section for residents and then on the main boulevard it became obvious that this was a party town by the number of bars we passed as we walked the main street. The competition must have been tough because there were signs in the windows advertising in English special drink deals. One sign said, "Rum and Coke – 15 pesetas", about 25 cents. We decided that we just couldn't pass up a bargain like that, so we walked in.

It was a huge bar and restaurant, lots of tables that were mostly empty because it was still early in the day. The guy behind the counter was a young American who explained that the bar was owned by an American and catered to mostly American, English and Northern European customers. We ordered our drinks and as he poured, he poured heavy. The drinks may have been inexpensive but there was a very liberal amount of rum in them. We drank our first round down and ordered another. The bartender had been in Sitges most of the summer and said the place was great for meeting young women on vacation and as he spoke I began visualizing what it must be like to be in his place, working a bar in this Spanish beach town, meeting tourist women and having mini affairs as they came and went. I decided there was probably nothing that a young guy could do that would be better.

As we got into our third round, I was so lost in the vision of this new fantasy that I began thinking again about not going back at the end of this trip. It occurred to me that I could come back to Sitges, get a job like this bartender and not go back to school and deal with a life that was not particularly fulfilling for me. But by then the tourist season would be over and as the bartender told us it pretty much dries up in the winter. Still, it was a wonderful thought. We ordered a fourth round and began to think that Sitges was a pretty good place after all. We came to the conclusion that we would stay and check out the night life.

Four Rum and Cokes in the middle of a hot afternoon initially makes a person a combination of happy, and bulletproof. Our attitudes were much more congenial than they had been last night and this morning, and it only cost us a dollar each. We walked back to

30

the beach, Sean was still sitting there, and he could tell immediately that we were feeling very good. He just laughed at us. Nothing like being sober around a couple of drunks; at least he was amused. We got our car and found another campground, by this time the hot sun and the rum were beginning to take its toll on us. It was time for a siesta.

When we woke it was getting dark and we were having second thoughts about going out to party some more. Somehow the appeal was not as great as it had been when we had that wonderful rum buzz. But we were committed so we went into town and got some food and then went back to our bar, it was definitely busier than it had been in the afternoon. We ordered another round of Rum and Cokes hoping we could re-capture the feeling we had earlier. The girls were pretty, but they were all attached. This all seemed to be a party and we felt a bit like outsiders. Even Sean didn't feel comfortable. We went to another bar and drank more of the same, but that magic was just not coming back. I made a mental note not to start drinking so early when the action takes place later in the night. We finally gave up about midnight and walked back to the campground and slept. The memory of Sitges was probably more imbedded in my soul than I realized at the time. It would be many years in the future that I would return and have a whole new appreciation of this beach town and the desire of wanting to stay and work, a decision that I would wonder if right or wrong on the long journey of my life.

Chapter 7

THE NEXT TWO days were spent driving. Our destination was Switzerland which was over 400 miles from Spain. As we passed through city to country to city again, we watched the changing landscape and felt the weather becoming cooler as we headed north. Spain was hot and dry as was southern France, but as we approached Lyon the countryside became greener. We mostly stayed on the highways but at times the highway would turn into two lane roads going through French villages.

Ever mindful of not spending too much money, we would stop at the little stores along the country roads to buy bread, cheese and ham or salami then sit by a stream eating and feeling the peace of nature. Then back through a city fighting traffic, getting lost and irritated. The ebb and flow, at peace with nature, then in turmoil in the city; I believe there was a lesson there. To me the city represents energy and excitement as well as dysfunction; the country is peace and harmony. Like the ego mind and the soul, I love them both as long as they are balanced.

By the second day we made it to the Swiss Border and crossed without incident. However, we forgot to stop for gas. Jerry was driving and both of us were thinking so much about getting to Zurich by evening that we completely forgot we had been driving all day without filling up. Driving along the autobahn the car began lurching and finally came to a stop as Jerry guided it to the side of the road.

There was absolutely nothing around but green fields, certainly no gas stations in sight. I volunteered to look for a gas station mainly because I had no patience for waiting. I took a path off the highway, not having any idea where I was going. It was a pleasant walk and I decided not to get stressed about the situation; after all, how often did I get to walk in the Swiss countryside. After about an hour I came to a quaint little village and saw there were a couple of gas stations, but they were closed. I had forgotten it was Sunday and it appeared in this little village there was not too much of anything open. I found a café/bar and walked in to ask for some directions to a gas station. Behind the bar a pretty woman in her late 20's looked up as I walked in. I asked her for directions, but she spoke no English and all I could get was that there were no stations open on Sunday.

Disappointed, I walked back to the autobahn about two miles past where the car was stalled and found an Auto Club call box. I pushed the button and a man came on the phone speaking what I presumed was Swiss. I tried to tell him we were out of gas, but he spoke no English, so I finally gave up figuring he didn't understand what I was trying to tell him. I decided to hitchhike to a gas station. I stuck my thumb out and got a ride from an Italian tourist who took me about 8 miles to a gas station. I realized if I had stayed on the main road the whole time, instead of going to that village I would have saved time, but then I would have missed the experience of walking to the village. I bought some gas in a can with the Swiss Francs I had exchanged at the border and was just about to hitchhike back when Jerry and Sean drove up with the car. Apparently, my call to the Auto Club triggered a location and a service vehicle was able to find the car by the side of the road. We gassed up and were on our way. I wondered if they ever would have found me if I had not gone to that gas station. Perhaps some things just need to go unsaid; it worked out, that was all that really mattered.

Since we had lost a couple of hours and it was nearly 5 in the afternoon, we decided it would be too late to go to Zurich, so we drove to Bern. Jerry and Sean wanted to camp another night, but I was at my limit, three nights of sleeping on the ground was enough, I wanted a bed. I told them to drop me off at a hotel and I would meet them later. We found a nice inexpensive hotel, so Jerry changed his mind and checked in with me. Sean decided he would just sleep in the car that night. It turned out to be a good decision, because it began raining that evening, and never stopped until morning.

Bern is a wonderful city and I was glad fate had brought us here. After we showered and changed, we went for a walk and found a restaurant. The menu was not in English, so I took a chance and ended up with pork chops which were delicious. After dinner we took a long walk as the rain began to fall. Watching the people in the streets of this elegant city I could see that the men and women were dressed in business attire and the whole scene looked very classy. I noticed one young man in a suit with a beautiful young lady on his arm as they strolled under their umbrella. They looked like a couple right out of a magazine ad and I longed to be that guy. Between the fantasy of Sitges and the sight of them, I was forming a vision for my life that would last forever.

There is a lifestyle of elegance that is appealing. and a far cry from the vagabond traveling, the hot Spanish sun and working in pubs and bars that was also appealing to me. I would spend most of my life trying to accomplish one or the other of these contrasting visions. I would succeed at times although I never appreciated it as much when I was in the picture myself; it always looks better when someone else is the actor, maybe it's because we have to take our own insecurities with us and it clouds our fantasy. The wonderful part of all this though, is I had a dream that would never let me accept status quo as a way of life. That would be a blessing and a curse, but the die was cast and there was no turning back.

After a wonderful night's sleep, I woke feeling better than I had in a long time. I had to force myself to wake at 8 but I didn't want to miss the breakfast that was included in the price of the room. Jerry and I walked down to the dining room where they were serving several kinds of rolls with butter that tasted like cream cheese, strawberry jam and coffee. It was all wonderful, especially the coffee which we hadn't had in a few days. We took a morning stroll, got Sean and then headed on to Lucerne.

Lucerne is also a beautiful city, smaller than Bern and not as modern but quite charming, a kind of stereotype of what you would expect in Switzerland. We walked around for a couple of hours looking at shops and exploring the city. I ended up buying a clock and a music box as gifts for my sisters. By 3 in the afternoon, we had seen enough of Lucerne and drove on to Zurich, which in contrast is a monster of a city. We decided in the short time we would be there; we wouldn't be able to see much so after walking around for an hour we drove on.

By 6 pm, it was raining heavily so we found a hotel near the road and checked in. As was the custom Sean would sleep in the car while Jerry and I stayed in the room. For Sean that was luxury, at least he didn't have to sleep on the ground which is pretty much what he did before he met us. Since it was still early, we sat in the covered patio of the hotel and drank beer while we discussed, and I'm sure solved most of the world problems. If only it were that easy.

The next morning, it was still raining. We had decided to go back to Garmisch on our way north to the Scandinavian Countries, Jerry wanted to get the car serviced and it would be good to see all the people one last time, especially Anne. We went back through Austria and then crossed the German border about two in the afternoon. We hadn't gone too far when a young guy on a motorcycle went flying by. Sean said, "that bloke is crazy; I doubt he will last long." People drive fast in Europe, especially in Germany but to drive that fast on a winding mountain road is asking for trouble. What is it that makes young people have very little fear? Sometimes I wonder how we make it to 30. I don't know if this "bloke" did because as we drove on, we saw the accident. It looked like he had been hit by a truck, probably crowded his lane on the turn. There was a small crowd of people gathered so there was no reason for us to stop; we couldn't add anything but confusion. As we drove past, I saw him move so I suspect he made it.

We got into Garmisch about 3 in the afternoon and found that Mac and Stephanie were not home. Jerry decided to drive up to the Lake, so Sean and I stayed and walked to the Hunter's Café, near their apartment, for a beer. About an hour later Jerry drove up with Mac and Stephanie. We introduced Sean to them and like us they took to him immediately. We barbequed steaks and then all went to the grill for a nightcap. I was hoping we would see Anne, but she wasn't there.

Mac and Stephanie had 3 extra places to sleep besides their own bed. One was a bunk bed that was a bit precarious when you had too much to drink, especially if you were on top, which I always was. Jerry usually slept on the lower bunk and there was a couch that Sean got since he had the least seniority at the apartment. Mac left for work in the morning and Sean and I got up and went for a walk while Jerry and Stephanie slept late. It was a gorgeous morning, the sky was blue the hills green, a perfect summer day. It is such a contrast from Spain to Switzerland and Germany

"Jerry's sis and husband are good people," I said.

"Yes, they seem like it," he responded, "did you know them before you came to Europe?"

"No, not at all. I really didn't know Jerry that well, we just got together because of the trip." I answered. "Speaking of trips, this last week must be different than the previous weeks you were traveling on the Continent."

"Quite so, I appreciate you and Jerry's generosity allowing me to travel with you." Sean said.

"You know," I began, "it really has added a lot to the trip. Probably because Jerry and I were not really close friends, it has been easy for the three of us to be together. Whatever reason, it works. I'm glad you are here Sean."

When Sean and I got back, Jerry and Stephane were up, and we decided to take care of business. We gathered all our very dirty clothes for a trip to the laundromat. We then set an appointment to get the car serviced and were disappointed to find we would have to wait 2 days. As usual I was anxious to get on the road, I don't know why, Garmisch was perfect and the friends of Mac and Stephane were becoming our friends. It was our home base so if we had to stay a couple of days, so what; it would be fun, that was guaranteed.

Mac only had to work until noon, so we decided to drive to Munich when he returned. Mac wanted to show us the city and then take us to the Hofbrauhaus. Munich is a sprawling modern city but still clings to German Folk history and is world famous for the Oktoberfest which takes place in the fall and brings millions of tourists to the city each year. We parked the car and walked a couple of blocks to the Hofbrauhaus a monstrous three story structure built in the 16th Century. When we entered the building, it reminded me of the beer fest we had gone to a couple of weeks ago except instead of a tent this massive building featured painted ceilings thirty feet high with enormous interior light fixtures hanging from the ceiling. Brass bands played polkas as stout waitresses brought liter mugs of beer six at a time. In addition to beer there was knockwurst and sauerkraut and hot pretzels to munch on. We had a great afternoon drinking and singing totally absorbed in the festive atmosphere. By the time the five of us walked out we were all laughing and enjoying the feeling of being alive or drunk depending on the perspective. We piled into Jerry's car with Mac driving and toured Munich for a while. There was too much to see in the time we had, so after an hour, we left Munich and drove back to Garmisch and the Grill.

When we walked in Anne was there, drinking with a group of people I didn't know. I was hoping she would be there and when she saw us and walked over, I was glad. We sat at a large table and ordered hamburgers and more beer. After dinner Mac and Stephanie got a ride home and Sean, Jerry, Anne and I stayed until the Grill closed at midnight. One of the barmaids there, Maggie, an American whose family was military, went with us to find another bar. By this time Sean had had enough and we dropped him off at the apartment. I guess being 25 he had more sense than us, but we were still feeling great and not ready to end the night. I am amazed that this little town has so many bars and pubs, but I suppose when you consider that there is a military base, there must be plenty of customers. Maggie directed us to a place called the Scotch Club. Anne had been drinking wine all night and as we sat in the bar it was obvious, she was going down for the count. Maggie and I began discussing the war in Viet Nam and got into a pretty heated debate. She was what we called then a hawk and of course I was considered a dove. Mixing alcohol and politics is always a recipe for an intense argument and it was clear that we did not like each other or each other's views. The discussion carried on over several drinks, Jerry was getting bored and Anne had finally passed out. We closed the bar half carried Anne to the car and dropped Maggie off. It still amazes me how either of us were able to drive. When we got back to the apartment Anne was out. Jerry and I managed to get her up the stairs and put her in his bed; he volunteered to sleep on the floor. What a guy.

One of the friends that hung around the group was Tim. He had been traveling for some time, living a life that I wanted to live. He had been stationed in Europe with the Army and when he was released, he just never went home. During the winter he worked the resorts on ski patrol and during the summer he worked at odd jobs and traveled. He had some great stories about his adventures while traveling. An excellent skier he had even done stunt work the past winter for the new James Bond Movie *Her Majesty's Royal Secret Service*. Today was his 26th birthday and everyone was planning a big surprise party for him. The plan was that he would come over to Mac and Stephanie's for tacos at six that evening and then we would take him to the Last Chance, another local American hangout, for drinks.

When we arrived, the gang was there yelling "surprise." He was quite surprised, and the party began. We literally took over the place. It seemed everyone knew Tim so even people not part of the party joined in. As I look back, I wonder how I was able to drink so late into the night the day before and then be up for partying again, but I didn't even consider slowing down. Tim had a very happy birthday, and when the party began to die down at the Last Chance; we drove over to the Grill. By this time Anne and I were hanging together pretty close. I liked being with her, even though she was so young, she was fun. I suppose I was just susceptible to her flirtations but with a few drinks in me I didn't care; I was just living for the moment and at this moment I was with her.

Once again, we closed the Grill. Jerry, Sean, Tim, Anne and I all got in Jerry's car and drove to the Lake where Tim was staying. We said goodbye; it was the last time I would see Tim and I was sorry; he was a cool guy. Saying goodbye is the hardest part of travel because you know that these people could be friends for a long time, but most likely I would never see them again. It is a microcosm of life, except that the time together is much quicker.

Anne continued to flirt, and I was eating it up. She kept telling me that she felt sorry that Jerry had slept on the floor so tonight she was going to sleep in my bed. I told her I wasn't sleeping on the floor so she would have to sleep with me, and she said she would. Of course, I didn't believe her, but I went along with the game. When we got to the apartment, I climbed up to my bunk fully clothed to see what she would do, she climbed in too. We were laughing about it because it was totally innocent. That night she slept with me, fully clothed

When I woke, I had to smile to myself at the situation, Anne was next to me asleep. As I lay there, I began to realize that we were leaving today, and I probably would never see her again. Another goodbye and this one would be the hardest yet. I woke her to let her know that there was no car to take her to work. Mac had followed Jerry to get our car that was being serviced so she would have to take the bus. I walked her to the bus stop which was just a couple of blocks from the apartment. Anne and I were never romantic but for the brief time we were together, we certainly liked each other. I would miss her.

As we waited for the bus, I said, "so we probably won't see you again."

"Where are you going next?" She asked.

"Driving north to see the Scandinavian Countries. I've always wanted to see them."

"Well, it was nice to get to meet you, it was fun," she said.

"It was, I will miss the time we had here, and I will miss you."

The bus was approaching, and she turned to me, "I'll miss you too." She looked up at me and we kissed. "Have a good life," she said.

I watched her step on the bus, one last look; a wave and she was gone.

Chapter 8

AT NOON WE got the car packed and said goodbye to Mac and Stephanie. I thought about all the people we had met in Garmisch, it was such a wonderful experience and it was hard to leave. I thought about Tim and I once again began to have daydreams of not going back home. The more I was in Europe the more I liked it. This was the happiest I had been in my life. There was the part of me that was spirited and yearned to be free. It was what took me to Newport Beach and what got me to Europe in the first place. But there was the part of me that was responsible and did what I "should." It was my own personal war. I was angry at myself because I knew I would go home, that I didn't have the guts to stay here. Besides there was the army and I would surely be drafted if I left school. Still, the thought just wouldn't go away.

We didn't get too far that day; drove through Munich and got almost to Nuremberg as evening fell. The partying the last two nights had finally caught up with us, we were tired, and a bit hungover, so we found a campground and were asleep by 9 that night.

Maybe my system was not cut out for drinking as much as I had in Garmisch. I had trouble sleeping and had bad dreams; then it began to rain in buckets. Jerry and I got in the car; Sean was sleeping under some trees. I slept until about 6:30 then got out of the car. It had stopped raining. Sean was awake so we walked to the camp store and got some coffee. When we came back to the car, Jerry was still sleeping. I didn't feel like waiting for him to wake up so Sean and I got in the front and I drove the car North through Nuremberg and on to Hamburg.

Hamburg is close to the northern border of Germany. We drove most of the day on the Autobahn and made good time. The speed limit was not enforced then, and we drove usually about 75 or 80 miles per hour. Of course, we were slow compared to the Germans who roared past us doing 100 or more. We saw one bad accident along the way, and I wondered if that was just normal for this area.

We arrived in Hamburg at about 4 in the afternoon. Our intention was to get tickets for the ferry that would take us to Denmark and then Sweden. Hamburg is the second largest city in Germany with well over a million people. The city was modern because most of it had to be rebuilt after the war. We drove in looking for a hotel so we could make reservations for the ferry, knowing that most of the hotels in the big cities have travel agencies. After making reservations, we drove to the port, where we were to pick up the ferry. We waited for about an hour for the next one to arrive; it was getting dark by the time we drove the car into the bowels of the ship. This was no small ferry it was like a miniature ocean liner. After parking the car, we looked for a place to get something to eat; we were starving. We found the dining room which had a huge circular food display. It was the first real hint that we were in a Scandinavian Country because laid out before us was a smorgasbord of food that was familiar, and some not so familiar. Most of it was good, however, I accidentally got some liver and thought I had been poisoned.

The dining room was crowded but we found a table near a group young people that looked American; which you can usually spot and since we are all travelers far away from home, there is a common bond that usually creates instant rapport. If we saw each other in Los Angeles, we wouldn't give a second glance. There were two girls who were sisters and a guy who had been going to school in Berkeley and fit the image. We shared travel stories and destination plans and ended up staying in the restaurant for the remainder of the trip.

When we reached port in Denmark, we all considered we should find a bar since none of us were ready to call it a night. The small town we landed in was called Gedsar. It wasn't much but we did manage to find a small pub where we could get beers and we continued our conversation about life and travel. The guy from Berkeley had some pretty liberal political views that made me look like I was conservative. He was a bit much for me and I made the decision that we would not travel with them past this night. It was getting late, so we followed each to a deserted location on the outskirts of town and camped for the night. It turned out to be one of the most miserable nights I had spent since arriving in Europe. We rolled out our sleeping bags about mid-night and the sky was so clear we could see a million stars. I awoke at 2 am as the rain came pouring down. I jumped up and tried to get in the car but couldn't because Jerry, bless his heart, had taken one of the girls in there with him and had the good sense to lock the doors. As I was getting drenched, I remembered I had an extra key in my pocket, so I opened the front door and sat in the passenger seat. I tried to sleep sitting up but only managed to catch bits of sleep through my discomfort of being wet and sitting up. About 5 am Sean was pounding on the door; he was tough but even he had given way to the down pour, so I let him in on the driver's side. Finally, at 6 the other girl had enough and got her sister away from Jerry and they all drove off. I took advantage of the empty spot and got in the back and slept for another few hours.

Feeling tired and edgy, we drove up to Copenhagen and caught the short ferry ride across to Sweden. We arrived in Landskrona and then drove north. It was still early afternoon, but we weren't up for driving anymore so we pulled into the first town we came to a place called Raa and got a hotel room. All I could do was drag myself to the bed and promptly fell into a deep four-hour sleep. When I awoke the room was empty so I went out to find the boys. They were sitting outside a small pub having a beer, I promptly sat down and joined them, feeling a bit more human and hospitable. None of us felt much like drinking and after one beer we decided to explore the town. There wasn't much to explore, we walked around the whole town 3 times in about a half hour. We finally bought a couple of English Magazines and went back to the room and read until Midnight.

I had always wanted to go to Scandinavia. I don't know if it was because I loved the Kirk Douglas movie, *The Vikings*, when I was a kid or because I had heard there were lots of beautiful women with very liberal ideas toward sex; probably both. Stockholm is 400 miles north-east of Raa and we decided to drive it in one day. The landscape as we drove north was a combination of forests and farmland and of course green and beautiful. Sweden has one of the highest standards of living in the world. Their government is somewhat socialistic with free medical services and generous pension programs, but the country is at the same time capitalistic and the combined system appears to work.

We got into Stockholm about four in the afternoon. The city was much bigger that I thought it would be, about a million people at that time, and of course the traffic was heavy like any big city. I had discovered that when coming to a city like Stockholm, that is so big and spread out and you don't have a clue where you are going, it is a bit unnerving trying to drive. Jerry was driving and he was not having a good time. We drove around for about an hour making our way into the center of the city where we located the main train station. That was the break we needed because there is usually travel and hotel directories in the train stations. This one was even better because there was a hostess that could arrange our accommodations. We of course were looking for the cheapest room we could find, and she located a room that was only four dollars a night per person. We had discovered by now that Sweden was expensive compared to other European Countries and realized, that was about the best we could do so we booked the room for three nights. Four dollars doesn't seem like much especially by current standards but when you are traveling on five dollars each a day, it pretty much blows out the budget.

Following the directions, we were given we drove to the address of the hotel. There was another surprise in store for us, absolutely no parking anywhere. After driving around several blocks near our destination I told them to drop me and the luggage off and I would check us in while they searched for a parking spot.

Finding the address, I opened the door expecting to see a check-in desk but instead all I found was a large hall with a stairway and an old-fashioned elevator. This wasn't a hotel it was an apartment building. Looking at the reservation slip I saw there was a number 5 so I figured our room had to be on the 5th floor. The elevator was just big enough for 3 people or me and the luggage, I pushed the number 5 and the elevator lurched upward, creaking and groaning. I wondered if this baby was going to make it up 5 floors. It did but at a speed that was slower than if I had walked up the stairs, wherever they were.

Our hostess was an old lady who didn't speak English but was able to show me our room which turned out to be just fine. It was nearly an hour before Jerry and Sean showed up, they found a parking garage a mile from our room and had to pay two dollars a night; another hit on the budget. The boys rested awhile and then we decided to explore Stockholm. We walked for about an hour in mostly residential neighborhoods but did manage to discover a pub and decided it was time for a beer. We ordered one for each of us and got our bill, 5.65 Croner, about $1.10 which was pretty good for three beers. Maybe Sweden wasn't so expensive after all. At least that's what we thought until we realized that the price was for one beer not three. We were all three in a state of shock and our faces must have been a sight to see because at one of the tables were two girls who started laughing at us.

They approached our table and one of them asked in English, "are you Americans?"

Jerry responded pointing to me, "he and I are American, Sean there is English."

One of the girls was blond with short hair and glasses that had started the conversation. She went on, "oh, we don't see many Americans around here."

I said, "would you like to join us?"

"Ok," she answered. They went to their table to get their drinks, came back and pulled two more chairs to the wooden table where we were sitting.

"My name is Lisa," the blond girl said, "and this is my sister Bret."

Bret in contrast to her sister, had long dark hair and I thought, if they were sisters, they looked nothing like each other. Through the conversation that followed we learned Lisa was 21, not very attractive but had a marvelous personality and somewhat flamboyant, where Bret, 19 was much quitter and down to earth.

For the rest of the evening we had a great time learning about Stockholm and exchanging stories of our countries. Europeans, especially those close to our age always were as curious about America as we were about their country. We were so absorbed in conversation that we didn't realize how late it was. Pubs in Sweden close at ten so we were politely asked to leave. We said good night and headed back to our room.

The next morning, I awoke early and went out to find some coffee. It was a beautiful August Morning and the bustle of the city was already present. I found a little café around the corner from our hotel and ordered coffee and a roll. It was good to get away and be alone, to reflect and write in the journal I was keeping. I drank my coffee and wrote while taking in the energy of the city.

After about an hour I walked back to the room and found Sean was awake. We had to sneak him in the room, and he slept on the floor, there was no way he could afford to pay the room rate and it was understood whenever we could help him out, we would. I had really grown to like Sean; he was easy to be around and because he came from a different life than Jerry and me, he offered a different perspective. Jerry was still sleeping so we went for a walk. Stockholm is like so many cities, located on a main waterway, which in this case feeds to the Baltic Sea. In the area we were staying it was mainly apartments and small stores, cafes and pubs. Stockholm has a large amount of high-rise apartment buildings mostly built after the war. We decided that if we were going to really see this city, we would have to take a bus because the size would not allow us to walk. It would be like trying to see Los Angeles walking.

Sean and I walked back to the room and woke Jerry, the day was wasting away, and I was anxious to explore. We took a bus down to the old section of the city on an island called Gamla Stan, (Old Town), where buildings 300 years old still stood. Gamla Stan was also the sight of the first palace built in the 13th Century. From there we walked to a different part of the city, the action spot, with clubs and bars. As we walked, I began to realize that the stories were true, the women were beautiful, one prettier than the next until after a while you just took it for granted. I do appreciate the architecture of the cities and it is interesting to see the old town and the development of the newer construction but for my money there is nothing that compares to a beautiful woman. My memory of Sweden is the women not the architecture.

We continued walking, block after block and eventually made our way back to our hotel. We climbed the 5 flights of stairs, which now was our routine, since the elevator was so slow. By the time we reached the top we were worn out. There was a vending machine in the hall that had sodas and beer, so we got three beers and sat in the room recuperating from the day.

Once we had recovered it was about six in the evening, so we headed out again for some dinner and then back to the action part of the city to check out the night life. We hadn't eaten all day except for a couple of rolls so we were starving as we walked into a neighborhood restaurant. The food was good, but we were all concerned with money, the rate we were spending in Sweden we would run out before the trip was over; we needed to get through the next day and get out of here. We walked to the nightclub area, but it was still much too early for any night life, which I figured didn't start until after ten. Feeling the pinch on our money we headed back to the room and called it an early night.

We came across a tourist book in the hotel that gave us information on restaurants, museums and discotheques, so in the morning we planned our last day in Stockholm. Our first stop was a restaurant that offered an all you could eat breakfast for a dollar. We were in heaven, there were eggs and rolls and butter, cereal and milk; it was our best find in Stockholm. Naturally we gorged ourselves deciding this would cover us until nighttime. Leaving the restaurant feeling good we walked to another island, (Stockholm is built on 14 islands), where we saw an old salvaged ship called the Wasa. As we walked out of the building it started raining bloody hell, as Sean would describe it, so we ducked into an Army Museum mainly to stay out of the rain. For someone who enjoys guns and cannons this was probably a very cool place but for me it was not interesting in the least.

It hadn't stopped raining by late afternoon, so we ended up taking a bus back to the hotel and sat down to plan our evening. Our tourist book explained that the discos didn't open until 9:30, so we figured we would go back to the local pub where we had met Lisa and Bret to kill some time before we went to the clubs. We ordered beers and were just finishing our first round when the two sisters walked in. They saw us and immediately walked to our table appearing happy that we were there. As we sat and talked I watched Lisa, she had teeth that were a bit crooked and with her glasses at first look she was rather plain, but as she spoke she was so full of life she had us all captivated. She was a lot of fun and seemed to have a knack of making each of us feel like we were special. I got the sense that this girl knew how to handle men and I was intrigued.

By ten I suggested we all go to the clubs, but the girls said no, they weren't up for it because they weren't dressed nice enough. I smiled to myself, this was universal; women worried about things like that, but of course we had no concern at all. Lisa suggested that instead we go to their apartment. We didn't need a lot of coaxing. We all walked out into the night and Lisa quickly latched onto my arm; this last night in Stockholm was looking like it had possibilities. The five of us walked to the girls' apartment, which took about an hour, but we were having fun. It had stopped raining and the night was beautiful. As I have mentioned, traveling is such a microcosm of life. Last night was totally dead, we were looking forward to getting out of Stockholm and now this evening we were having a wonderful time. We also had made plans for something totally different, but fate had given us something better and we were flexible enough to allow that change to happen. It seemed that as we went from day to day and adventure to adventure there was good and bad; but the good was very good.

We arrived at the apartment and Bret asked if we would like some tea. The apartment was very small and looked like a typical American College Student's except the furniture was Swedish Modern which to me was very unusual. As we were settling down, Lisa seemed to lose interest in me and started getting close to Sean. That was quick; I guess when traveling another rule is, make your decisions fast because there isn't much time for long courtships. Bret and I began talking as she made the tea for everyone.

"How long have you and Lisa been living here," I asked.

She looked up from her project and I found myself staring into beautiful light blue eyes that I had not paid attention to before. "We moved in a little over a year ago, actually, when I turned 18. We are from a smaller town north of Stockholm called Falun. My father is a manager of a mining company and my mother is a nurse. Lisa and I wanted to see the big city and we love it here; it really is exciting," she said enthusiastically, "after living in a small town." Bret continued, "Lisa is a licensed nurse. She got a job at the hospital here and found one for me as a receptionist and clerk.

"Are you going to become a nurse like Lisa and your mother?"

Bret poured five cups of hot tea into little cups, placed them on a tray while telling me "No I don't think so. I'm not crazy about the medical field. I'm going back to school and hope to get my degree," she giggled, "maybe I can decide what I want to do."

She was very pretty with long brown hair and blue eyes and seemed to have a depth to her that Lisa was missing. It always amazes me how siblings can be so different. These two were night and day. For me it would be a preview to my life in the future; attracted to the wild spirited personality but always more comfortable with the sensible one. The conflict was part of the duality of my own personality.

"Do you miss your family?" I said.

"Yes sometimes, but we go home every month"

She carried the tea into the living room, and I followed her. Sean and Lisa were getting cozy on the couch and Jerry was looking bored with the whole situation. I sat down on the last remaining chair and Bret sat next to me on the floor. Jerry drank his tea in two gulps, got up and announced he was leaving. I knew he was trying to help us out by evening the odds. He was off on his own adventure alone. The rest of the night the four of us sat and talked. It was a bit awkward with the two couples trying to get to know each other sitting in this tiny living room but the time slipped away and soon it was 2 am. The girls had to work the next day so we finally said goodbye not knowing if we would see them again. It was raining again, hard, so we decided to take the subway back to the hotel. On the way back we talked about staying another night, seemed a shame to let these girls go, but we figured Jerry would want to leave.

Little did we know that Jerry had discovered the night life we had been seeking for the last 2 nights and found it to be to his liking. He had met a lady from Finland at a club and was now in love and wanted to stay another night. It was settled. Once again just when we were planning to leave a place it started to get good. I was glad we didn't have a rigid itinerary.

I woke up later than I planned; I didn't want to miss that one-dollar breakfast that was over at 10 am. Sean was already gone, Jerry was asleep, so I scrambled out of bed and got to the restaurant by 9:30. Sean was waiting for me; he had finished his breakfast and was drinking coffee as I joined him. Besides the evening with Bret and Lisa and drinking at the pub, this breakfast was the highlight of Stockholm. I suppose you could consider us very unsophisticated, scorning museums and tourist attractions for women, booze and cheap food, but as far as I was concerned, Europe was about merging with the cultures rather than knowledge of the history.

Our morning was busy with necessary adjustments to our original plan. We walked back to the hotel and I managed to communicate to the owner that we wanted to stay one more night. She was agreeable and we got to look forward to another day of climbing five flights of stairs every time we came or went. Jerry finally woke and we all headed to the car to pay another day's rent at the garage. We had to get more Kroner's to spend another couple of days in Sweden, so we found a bank and exchanged some money. It occurred to us that our ladies didn't know we were going to be here another day, nor did we know if they even cared. But it was worth a chance, so we took the subway to their apartment to leave a note suggesting they meet us at the Pub at 7:30.

We were there by 7:00 wondering if they would come. At 7:30 they had not arrived and by 7:45 we figured it was not going to happen. Before we could start feeling foolish for staying another night, they walked in. Jerry left to find his Finish lady and we ordered beers for the four of us. As the evening wore on Lisa and Sean were becoming quite romantic and finally about 9:30 they headed out, I presumed to the apartment to be alone. Bret and I stayed and talked, she was growing on me and I thought it was a shame she didn't live in Newport, it would be nice to have someone like her as a girlfriend. For 19 Bret was mature and quite different than American girls I had known.

"Tell me about California, I would like to go there sometime. I have read about it and it seems fantastic." She said.

"It is pretty amazing," I told her. "Where I'm from is an agricultural town in Central California. My grandfather lived in Newport Beach which is a very special beach town and so when I went to college, I moved there. Probably not great for a serious student, but really, I don't like school anyway."

"Really?" She asked in a shocked voice; "I love school. So you moved to the beach because your grandfather is there."

"Was there," I replied. "He died a few years ago. I moved there because I love the town and like you, I wanted to get out of the small town and living with my parents."

"How old are you?" She asked.

"I just turned twenty-two this summer".

"Are you going to finish college?"

"Probably. Even though I don't like it, I don't want to get drafted in the army and fight in a war I don't believe in."

We then got into a discussion about the Viet Nam War. Most Europeans that I talked to except Maggie in Garmisch, were against that war. It always elicited a lively discussion.

At 10 the Pub closed so we left and took the long walk back to her apartment. As we walked, I put my arm around her shoulder, and she responded by putting her arm around my waist. The night was clear, the stars glittering, we stopped to look and then I kissed her. I looked into her eyes, it was a freeze frame moment in time, one of those where the rest of the world could go away I didn't care I was content being with her and I didn't want the night to end. We continued walking arm in arm and I thought about how just 24 hours ago I was walking like this with her sister. I was glad it had turned out the way it had.

By the time we got to the apartment Sean and Lisa were sitting in the living room talking. Bret and I joined them but both girls were tired and had to work again the next day so we told them we would probably meet them again the next night and left. On the subway back Sean said that Lisa was a tease and he really had no interest in seeing her anymore. I felt different; I liked Bret and wanted to spend more time with her.

We got back to the hotel about 1 am, Jerry was not back. I lay in bed thinking about Bret. If we stayed, there was nothing to do during the day; we were getting bored with Stockholm. Sean was done with Lisa and who knew what Jerry was up to? One more day wouldn't matter, I would never see her again whether the last time was this night or the next. As I made my decision, I already was beginning to miss her.

Jerry stumbled into the room about 5:30 the next morning. His Finish girl friend had stood him up, so he ended up going to the nightclubs again and apparently had a good time, he had spent all his Swedish money. Sean and I let him sleep while we went for a $1 dollar breakfast. We decided we would leave and after breakfast we took one last walk around the city. Jerry slept until noon and would have kept sleeping if we hadn't forced him up. I went to get the car while he was clearing his head and we finally left Stockholm at three that afternoon. I wanted to stop and drop a note at Bret's apartment, but Jerry was in no mood, so we didn't. As we drove out of the city I wondered if they would show up at the Pub and how would Bret feel when we weren't there. We never really said good-bye.

Chapter 9

FOR THE NEXT 5 nights we visited Oslo, Norway and Copenhagen, Denmark driving over 600 miles. As we left Stockholm, I realized that our trip was over two-thirds complete. My money also was about two-thirds gone and we realized that we would need to be frugal if we wanted it to last to the end. We had saved money in Garmisch, but Stockholm was a bit of a blowout moneywise. One way to cut back on expenses was to not drink the way we had in Garmisch. Not quit, mind you, a casual beer or two at night would be fine.

It was approximately 250 miles from Stockholm to Oslo Norway, our next destination and if we had left early enough we would have made it that day, but we were tired so after two hours of driving we stopped for dinner which consisted of Hotdogs, Fries and a Coke. Not very Swedish but it was good, even had ice-cream cones for dessert. We drove on; the road seemed to be carved right out of the forest because Pine trees were all we could see on either side. By eight we pulled into a small turn out along the road and dug out one of the cans of Stew that we still had from Garmisch. We cooked it on the Sterno and after eating tried to come up with a plan for the evening. It was still too early to go to sleep, after all it was Friday night so we thought we would drive into a town and find a Pub. It took us about 30 minutes to see a sign that said Okna 6 km. We turned down the road which after about 3 kilometers turned to dirt. Driving on we began to wonder what kind of town this would be. We finally saw the sign Okna. There was one house and just past the house was a sign going the other way announcing Okna. This was the smallest town I had ever seen. After collaborating on what just happened, we decided the place was so desolate that they named towns after the people who owned the land and the government erected road signs so their relatives could find them. Not to be discouraged from our quest to find a Pub on Friday Night we drove back to the main road and carried on north until we saw another sign, Helna 4 km. This had to be it; we turned and drove a couple of kilometers but began to realize we were going to have the same luck as the road turned to dirt. We soon learned that Okna was not the smallest town we had ever seen because Helna was. There was no house, only a sign announcing Helna and on the other side of the sign Helna again. A double-sided sign: we were sure we had just driven into the "Twilight Zone." By this time, it was nearly ten, so we drove back to the main road, found a turn out and camped for the night.

I woke up and it was light so I looked at my watch; 4:30 am, how could it be so light? I didn't realize at the time that we were nearly at the 60th parallel which was almost as far north as Alaska. There was not a whole lot of darkness this time of the year. I went back to sleep for another three hours before we hit the road again. It took us most of the morning to get to the Norwegian border, and we drove into Oslo about 2 in the afternoon. Of course, our first stop was the train station where we booked a room for $2 a night which was better than the price in Stockholm. We got an overview of the city on the map we had picked up at the train station. Oslo is smaller than Stockholm, with less than half a million population at that time. The city did not have the number of high-rise apartments that many of the large European cities had, but they did have a very modern city with a high standard of living.

We walked down to the harbor and strolled along the waterfront. It was quite beautiful in the early evening. As we were walking, we came to a restaurant, so we went in and had a beer. While we were there, we learned from the waiter that most Norwegian clubs would not allow us to enter without ties. Can you imagine us vagabonds with ties on? That wasn't going to happen. We left the restaurant wondering what we were going to do when a couple of young Norwegian guys walked by and we asked if they knew of any bars we could get into. My experience with Europeans, especially those our age was they were very hospitable. They don't just tell you; they show you. They walked us to a place called King George, an English style pub. We spent the rest of the evening drinking beer and talking.

It was the last day of August which gave us a little more than a week before we would have to fly home. I didn't even want to think about it. The weather in Oslo the next day was beautiful, 70 degrees with not a cloud in the sky. We decided to take advantage of it and see the sights. There were three ways to get to the museum from our room, bus, ferry or walk. We decided to walk, and it turned out to be a good decision. It was three miles but a pleasant walk through the city and then a path through the woods. A museum with a Viking Ship was very interesting to me although I was amazed that all the furniture was so small. These people were little compared to us. I just visualized the Vikings as bigger than life. We then saw Thor Heyerdahl's Kon Tiki and then a war ship called the Fram.

By mid-afternoon we had seen all we wanted so Jerry and I took the ferry back and Sean walked. We spent the rest of the afternoon reading about what we had seen that day. That evening since we had already determined our options for night life was limited, Jerry and I decided to go to a movie. We had walked by a theater earlier and had seen there was a 7 pm showing of the "Guns of the Magnificent 7" a sequel to the original movie. Sean decided to stay at the room and read. The evening was nice as we walked to the theater. It was a modern version of our old theaters with only one screen but a nice large lobby with the traditional snack bar. It seemed that it was a big attraction because when we arrived the 7 o'clock showing was sold out. We decided to come back for the 9 pm showing and have some dinner. When we came back the crowd had thinned out and we got in. The movie was good but what I liked was that it was in English with Norwegian subtitles.

Copenhagen, Denmark is only about 300 miles from Oslo if you go straight down the channel but we didn't want to spend the money for that long ferry ride so we drove down the west coast highway of Sweden which probably added an extra hundred miles to the journey. We drove all day and got to the ferry by 7 pm but chose not to cross because we didn't want to look for a room in a new city late at night. We found a bar and had a couple of beers then drove outside of the town and found a good place to sleep off the road.

Sean and I woke up early and walked to a bakery where we bought rolls, butter and milk, our typical roadside breakfast. Jerry was up by the time we got back, and we drove to the shorter ferry crossing from Sweden to Denmark. Copenhagen is only 30 miles from the ferry port, so we arrived early and made our usual quest to the main train station. The city of Copenhagen is the major seaport of Denmark as well as the cultural and economic center. The city itself was about half a million and very modern, but also had charming older housing similar to Holland. At the train station we booked a room for $2 a night each in a private home.

Our hostess was not very friendly, she spoke no English and I figured she either just didn't like renting rooms to young guys like us but needed the money or she just was naturally uptight. The room was nice and clean as well as cheap, so we didn't give it a whole lot of concern. We parked the car and walked around the city. It is spread out like Stockholm, so it is difficult on foot to see everything. We walked to the harbor and saw the famous statue of the Little Mermaid, which is a tribute to Denmark's native son, Hans Christian Anderson. As the day wore into evening, we were getting hungry, so we took a bus back to the train station where we had seen an inexpensive restaurant.

The train station was near the main square of town and surrounding the square were office buildings and hotels. Across from the station was the Tivoli, one of the main tourist attractions of Denmark. We wanted to check it out and found it was like a combination of Disneyland and a county fair. As it became dark the Tivoli was beautiful with an array twinkly lights throughout the park. We walked around listening to bands and drinking beer. There were slot machines, but we weren't ready to part with our money gambling.

51

While we were walking, I began telling Jerry that if they had a place to ring the bell with the hammer, that I could do it. It was the beer talking, but there didn't appear to be one around, so I didn't have to worry about being tested. Wrong again, and as we approached the bell, I was sorry I had said anything. Standing in front, Jerry challenged me to make good my boast. There were lots of people around and I didn't want to do it, but I had no choice, my mouth had written a check my actions needed to cash. So, I told him, "If I ring the bell you pay for it, if not I'll pay for it". He agreed, he was quite sure I wouldn't do it. I remembered when I played golf that before hitting the ball, it was best to concentrate and visualize hitting it square then right before swinging getting that feeling of serenity. So, I visualized, relaxed and then swung with all the strength I had. The bell rang and I was as surprised as Jerry.

The following day was our last day in Denmark and our plan was to visit the Carlsberg Brewery. Exporting beer is one of Denmark's big industries and a tour of the Carlsberg Brewery is a popular tourist attraction. Of course, for us it was a must see since we were far more interested in beer than art and we heard that you got to sample the products.

As usual Sean and I had woken before Jerry and walked to a bakery for coffee and rolls. When we got back to the room Jerry was still asleep, so we woke him, the tour began at 10:30. We walked to the brewery and got in line for the English-speaking tour. We marched through the plant looking at the spotlessly clean machinery and learning the art of making beer. It was interesting but the best part was the end as we assembled into a large hall to be treated to pitchers of beer. There were quite a few Americans on the tour, all of them older than us. We sat at a table with a couple from Oregon who were on a 30-day tour of Northern Europe. By their appearance I'm sure they were not staying in a two dollar per night room like we were. They weren't that interested in drinking beer at 11:30 in the morning so we drank their share out of the pitcher on the table. We stayed as long as we could, enjoying the hospitality but finally it was time to leave and make room for the next group.

We spent the next few hours, after leaving the Carlsberg Brewer walking the city, but because of the early beer we soon decided to go back to the room and nap. My intention was to sleep for an hour but when I awoke it was four hours later. Sean had gone out and returned already, Jerry was just coming to. Maybe we drank more than we thought. After shaking out the cobwebs, we left the room to find some food. We took a bus into the main part of town and found a cheap restaurant. After eating we found a place called Club 6 that had a live band. The music was good but there were not many people in the bar, especially women. Probably because of the long nap we ended up staying until 2 in the morning and then discovered there were no buses running at that time; we would have to walk. It took us an hour and a half to get to our room and this walk was not nearly as much fun as the one we had earlier in the day. It was after 3:30 by the time we got to bed.

Chapter 10

WE WERE COMING to the end of the trip; only a few days left, and we weren't sure where to go next. We thought about Berlin, but we would have to pass through East Germany which meant getting a visa. I would learn later that we could have just driven to West Berlin. We did want to spend more time in Amsterdam so we finally concluded that we would spend only a couple of days in Germany going down to Frankfurt before we went back up to the Netherlands.

We left Copenhagen and drove to the ferry that would take us back to Germany. We had to wait a couple of hours before we could board because we hadn't made a reservation. When we finally got on, we went straight for the smorgasbord. A big meal was what I needed and after gorging on the great array of food from the buffet, I was feeling much better.

By the time we disembarked from the ferry back in Germany it was 3:30. It would be 300 miles to Frankfurt, so we made the decision not to drive all the way this day. We drove for the rest of the afternoon and into the evening but Jerry and I were both tired from the small amount of sleep we had the night before and finally we pulled off the autobahn and into an auto and truck rest stop. There was a cafeteria, so we had a light dinner then parked the car near a grassy area. I rolled out my sleeping bag and was asleep by 9 o'clock.

It was a long night. Trucks rolled in and out continuously, making sleep difficult. Finally giving up as the new day dawned, we drove on to Frankfurt arriving about 11 in the morning. Frankfurt is the financial capital of Germany and a popular tourist destination. I found it to be a much warmer city than Hamburg. Maybe it was the places we visited while in those cities, but it just had a better feel to me. We bought some knockwurst and rolls from a vendor at a large park and walked until we found a place to sit. It was nice just relaxing and watching the people as we ate our lunch. There were busy businesspeople, grabbing a quick bite to eat before heading back to work and there were older folks in no particular hurry, probably because like us they had no place they had to be at any particular time. There were the young lovers, walking hand in hand and to me they were the best of all. There is something about seeing people in love that makes other people feel good. We sat eating our food, enjoying the atmosphere and feeling content. The people here were the same as they were in the U.S. They had the same problems, same heartaches, same happiness, laughter and tears, yet 25 years before another generation was killing each other. How can that make sense? Each country killing young men under the banner of patriotic duty and now we were doing the same thing in Viet Nam, I thought. People, that years later, we would be friends with. War is just insane, the result of ego driven maniacal leaders and politicians. I thought about those guys my age fighting in South East Asia. I felt guilty that I was here in peace, traveling and having the time of my life while they were entrenched in a war, they could not win for a country that wouldn't support their sacrifice. What a shame.

We sat for an hour or so then moved on. I wanted to buy some gifts for my parents and my grandmother. We strolled around the city and I found some nice things that I thought they would enjoy but have no recollection of what it was. As the day was turning to evening, we went back to our car and drove out of the city to a campground. It was still light, so we got the Frisbee we had picked up in Garmisch and threw it until it was too dark. As the sun was going down, I looked out at the countryside, it was so green and beautiful, I was constantly amazed at the beauty of this country.

At the camp store we bought some bread and ham for dinner and picked up a bottle of Jägermeister which Jerry and I drank while we ate. Sean was not interested in the liquor. After we ate, we walked to the little bar restaurant and drank beer and played some slot machines. I wasn't going to drop too much money in them but on my third coin I hit a jackpot. Not a big one but enough for us to order a plate of French fries. We sat and talked for a couple of hours.

Jerry commented, "we are going to have to go to Rotterdam to deliver the car to the company that will ship it to California."

Sean looked at the two of us and said, "I believe that is where I will leave you blokes."

"This is it?" I said.

"It makes sense. I'm nearly out of money, just enough to catch a train to Den Haag and a ferry to London."

I didn't want to think about it. Time was closing in on us. The weather was changing; it was cooler now with summer almost gone. Sean had stayed on the Continent longer than he planned because of us. It had been his good fortune to meet us, but it had been ours as well. We had one more beer while we discussed the trip. I shook off the desire to be nostalgic and we laughed about some of our adventures – how good it would be to bottle it up forever – but now, it was coming to an end.

In the morning we awoke and headed for the Netherlands. It had been cold last night but fortunately my sleeping bag was warm. It was the last night I would sleep outside. On that crisp September morning: the next day, we set out for our final destination, Rotterdam where Jerry would have the car shipped back to the States. We arrived in Rotterdam late in the afternoon. Jerry and I found a room for the night, Sean decided to sleep in the car because we couldn't sneak him in our room. We walked around the town for a while and then Jerry and I went to the hotel and read until midnight.

The next day was busy. We cleaned out the car, packed all our clothes, gifts and souvenirs into suitcases and put the cases in a locker at the train station. We then drove to a car wash because we were told they would not ship the car dirty. Finally, Jerry drove the last couple of miles to the shipping company, filled out the necessary papers and left the car; then we took a taxi back to the train station.

Sean had just enough money to get home, so he bought a ticket to Den Haag. I think we spoiled him, because he didn't want to hitchhike. It appeared he was ready to go home. How do you say goodbye to a brother? We would never see him again, even though we didn't know it at the time I sensed it. Sean was as much a part of the trip as Jerry. Fate had brought us together as fate does in life and as someone wrote once; some for a reason, some for a season and some for life. Our paths cross, we experience time together then the path takes us in different directions. I would miss him and saying goodbye was difficult. Jerry and I were taking the train to Amsterdam and it was time to go. We shook hands and he walked away. Our friendship was for a season, but I believe also, for a reason.

Chapter 11

WE ARRIVED IN Amsterdam late in the afternoon; I called the ladies at the Hotel Bierenbroodspot to see if they had a room. Lotte, the mother said yes, not only was there a vacancy, but we could have the same room and they were excited that we were back. Loading our luggage into a taxi we took a wild ride to the hotel. Jerry and I looked at each other as we got out of the car, I don't think this guy had brakes, I was grateful we made it alive. Lotte ad Sophie were waiting for us; we told them we would be there for three nights before flying home. We visited for about an hour, telling them of the countries we had visited and some of the people we met. They were kind of like our parents away from home and very interested in our travels.

Finally, Jerry and I put our cases in the room, cleaned up a bit and then took an electric tram to the center of town. We walked to a Wimpey's for dinner then explored the city at night. Amsterdam is a city that is very much alive no matter what night it is. We walked by some night clubs, but we weren't in the mood, we just wanted to find a nice comfortable bar with good music. We walked into a place that was perfect. The music was playing, and it wasn't crowded so we found a table easily. We ordered a couple of beers and talked about what we would do the last couple of days. There were plenty of tourist attractions we wanted to see, so we knew it would be a matter of choices. By 10 o'clock we took the tram back to the hotel and went to bed early.

We woke and had our breakfast of eggs, pastries, juice and coffee then set out to explore Amsterdam by day. Amsterdam without question was my favorite city. It is quaint and serene with the canals and architecture, yet the night life has something to offer for everyone and every taste. In addition, the people of Amsterdam are the friendliest in Europe.

Our first stop was the Ann Frank house, which turned out for me to be depressing; seeing the home where she and her family had hidden from the Nazi's. I have a hard time understanding this aspect of human nature. While it is admirable that she had such a wonderful spirit and is truly a testimonial to a young positive mind, in all of my life I have never figured how other humans could use the excuse of following orders to send innocent people away from their homes to death camps. Nor do I understand doing so because of their religion or ethnicity. I could understand why the generation of adults in Holland, my parent's age, had such a disdain for Germans.

Next, we went to the Rijksmuseum which displayed the art of Holland's native son Van Gogh. At the time it was hard to appreciate the significance of the art because I had never studied the history of the impressionist artists or the tragedy of Van Gogh's life. Still, the art left an imprint on my memory and years later I would remember these pieces when I read and understood more about it.

We had one more stop that afternoon, the Heineken Brewery. Even though we had already been to the Carlsberg Brewery we weren't going to miss this one. Through our travels we had encountered other travelers who said Heineken was a must see. As it turned out they were right. Blend the hospitality of the Dutch with what some consider the world's best beer and you have a great tour and a pleasant post tour party. This time, however, we only had a couple of beers, not enough to get us into trouble.

It was late afternoon; we jumped on to the now familiar tram and went back to our hotel to get ready for the evening. Our intention was to have dinner then go to a dance club. While Jerry was taking a shower, I asked our hostesses, who always seemed to be together, about the restaurants in Amsterdam.

Sophie said enthusiastically, "oh you are going to find every kind of cuisine in Amsterdam, because we have every kind of culture here."

Lotte continued the dialogue saying, "Have you had Chinese here yet?"

I shook my head and said "no, we saw a few while walking around."

"Well then, that would be a good choice. There are many Chinese Restaurants and most are inexpensive."

"Great suggestion," I said.

Stepping off the tram, at Dam Square, we walked until we saw a restaurant that looked good. Since the menus are posted on the outside, we could see that the prices were not out of range. We went in and had one of the best Chinese meals I had ever experienced. Leaving the restaurant feeling full, content and in good moods we began walking. As we approached the corner and stopped for a signal, Jerry said, "Oh my God, look." I turned to look and there it was, across the street was the famous red-light district. We had heard so much about the prostitutes of Amsterdam and how the government watched over the legal operation and how the girls would sit in windows allowing the customer to window shop before deciding. They called it De Wallen. We had heard it was amazing, beautiful women on display like they were mannequins in a dress shop and each available if you were willing to pay. We had talked about this throughout the trip. Should we do it? Would we?

We walked into a bar and had a beer, discussing the situation. There was a conflict. In California buying a girl was not a cool thing to do. It was cheating if you had to pay for it. Yet in Europe prostitution was accepted for what it was. In fact, in another era, young men were encouraged to gain their experience with a prostitute rather than taking advantage of young girls.

"The way I see it, while we are here, we need to do it, we won't get another chance after we leave. It's part of the whole experience of Amsterdam" Jerry said.

"Yeah, like going to the museum." I commented sarcastically.

"Come on you know you want to; it will be an adventure."

He was right, I did want to, but what I wouldn't admit to him was I was scared. This was like deciding to go for a parachute jump; I got nervous just thinking about it. As we drank and talked, we became more determined that we would do it. Of course, when there are two young men on a course that is daring, there is the element of pride that will not allow you to change your mind. Once we said we would do it, we had to do it. That was the resolve that we created as we sat there.

"Tomorrow night" Jerry said. "Our last night; what a way to go."

We left the bar and walked to a disco club. The music was loud and the energy high. It was packed with young people drinking and dancing, a big party. Jerry and I were the same; neither of us were smooth nor had lines that allowed us to meet ladies, in fact we were both very shy. The girls almost had to approach us if we were going to meet them. That was why it was good to have Sean with us; he had more bravado. I had friends in California that would walk into a place like this and have a woman within the hour. We, on the other hand, lacked that ability, so we stood and drank as we watched the party around us.

When I was first out of high school, I had a good friend say to me, "why are you so afraid of women, you are so brave with everything else". He was referring to the fact that I could climb a 3-meter diving board and attempt a two and a half, (two and a half somersaults); flop, hurt myself and get back up and do it again. I didn't have a lot of fear, just enough to keep me from getting killed, but when it came to women, I had no guts at all.

After about an hour we had enough of the disco. There was no place to sit and we were tired of standing around like wall flowers. As we walked out our conversation went back to De Wallen and the next day, our last night. I felt a combination of excitement and dread.

I woke later than normal. I had slept well, and it was very comfortable in our Amsterdam quarters, very much like home away from home. Jerry and I had made no plans other than our evening adventure. We had breakfast then set out for the day. Instead of taking the tram downtown we just began walking. This neighborhood, the same one we had walked the first night we were here nearly six weeks before was still enchanting to me. Block after block of brick apartments with quaint little gable roofs.

Eventually we came to a neighborhood block of stores and found a small bookstore. We figured we would buy a book then go to a park and read. Fortunately, there was a good selection of paperbacks in English. I bought JD Salinger's" Catcher in the Rye", Jerry bought a science fiction novel. We kept walking, stopped at a market to buy some rolls, cheese and ham for later then found a little park that was along-side a pond and spent the rest of the day reading. It was a wonderful late summer day; the weather was beautiful with just a trace of crispness in the warm sun filled sky. There were swans gliding effortlessly in the pond and I thought of Hans Christian Anderson and his story of the Ugly Duckling. It always has been one of my favorite stories because all of us are swans in some way, but we often find ourselves in an environment that does not allow us to appreciate our better qualities. One of the hardest lessons for young people and often older as well, is learning to find the qualities within you that resonate with your soul and then have the courage to follow through. When you are a swan in a pond of ducks you can never actualize yourself; you will always feel less than whole. I felt a lot like that at times but here in Europe I was in the swan lake. I was at home here; I don't know why. I was not at home in college; I never had been comfortable in school. But was it really Europe or was it the freedom? I don't know but either way it was a good place to be.

The day wore on; we kept reading and talked, mostly about the night ahead. Every time I thought about it, I got nervous; I wanted to do it but then again, I didn't and probably wouldn't if Jerry was not there to ridicule me for being chicken. He probably felt the same way but never said so. Around 5 o'clock we left the park and took the long walk back to the hotel.

While Jerry was taking a shower, I sat in the room still reading and thinking about our last night. I probably would get melancholy about it except I had too much anticipation for what was left. I took my shower next and we got ready for the evening. As we walked out Lotte and Sophie said good night and wished us a "very nice evening". I smiled; I felt like we were off to rob a bank. I wondered what they would think if they knew what we were planning.

We took the tram into the city. By this time, we knew the route by heart. For our last dinner we went to an Italian Restaurant close to the bar we had been, our first night back in Amsterdam. The food was good, I had tortellini Jerry had spaghetti and we ate lots of bread. After dinner we took the short walk to our bar. The night was alive even though it was a Tuesday Night, but then every night seemed like a Saturday Night in Amsterdam. There was an electricity that you could feel as you walked along the sidewalks and canals. We stepped into the bar, it was still early so there were plenty of tables and we chose one of the bar tables, sat down on and ordered beers. The music was good; Stones, Led Zeppelin, some old Cream and Beatles. Honky-tonk Woman by the Rolling Stones was the current hit and we couldn't get enough of it. It had been another of our theme songs for the trip.

While we were sitting there enjoying the music and beer, two guys walked in who were obviously Americans and sat at a table near us. I asked them how long they had been in Amsterdam. One of them answered, "We just got in today; this is our first night."

I felt we were passing the torch, their first night our last. We invited them to our table and introduced ourselves. The tall one was named Rob the other, shorter with glasses, was Mike. They were older than us, probably in their late 20's and were from Texas. Rob had been to Amsterdam before when he was in the service. He and his buddy had planned this trip, but they only had a couple of weeks. As we drank and talked, we told them of our plan to go to De Wallen. Rob said, "Great, can we go with you?" They had planned to go there anyway at some point in their vacation so why not tonight.

So here we were, four Americans on holiday, in Amsterdam looking for adventure with the women of the streets. We must have had a half a dozen rounds, I lost track, but as we walked out of the bar, we were all feeling very good. It was a classic scene, the four of us walking; weaving would be a more appropriate description, laughing and goading each other as we approached our destination. Of course, they didn't know it, but I couldn't shake my fear, I wanted to back out but couldn't, the closer we got the more scared I became.

De Wallen, at the time was two or three blocks of girls some in windows some just standing by a door. Like any retail store there are better locations than others and I'm sure it was based on cost, seniority and who you knew. The four of us walked around getting a feel for the area and looking at the girls most of whom were quite beautiful. Deciding would be difficult. We walked around a couple of times before Rob suggested that we split up. It was too uncomfortable to walk up to a girl with the whole group watching. It was almost 10 o'clock we would meet at this spot at 11. Everyone agreed, and we all set off in different directions. By this time my heart was pounding; this was it.

I hung back for a while letting Jerry and the Texans get away from me then I started walking. The girls were friendly, smiling, beckoning but I just couldn't force myself to walk up to any of them. I must have walked around for 45 minutes and realized I was running out of time. I had to do this, one more pass and I would choose. Then I saw her. I had just passed the main block and on a side street she stood smoking a cigarette. I don't know why but she looked nice, not hard or painted up and I felt a bit more at ease as I approached her.

Her name was Marta; she had light brown hair that fell to her shoulders, with just enough wave to give it style. Her eyes were hazel and as I looked in them there was an intense combination of kindness and pain that was hidden by a radiant smile. It was a smile that said my life has not been kind, but I can still enjoy my life even if it is just for the moment.

I was scared and she knew it. My first words were "Do you speak English?" She answered yes.

"How much?" I really had no idea.

"Twenty guilders," about five dollars.

I said "ok" and she opened the door and we walked in. I must have looked like some scared animal to her. She could have taken advantage of that and of me because as it turned out I was unable to perform; I was just too nervous. She had my money all she had to do was say to me, "sorry" and send me on my way. She went to the back of this tiny apartment that was no more than the room we were in right off the street, a kitchen and a bathroom, and brought back some coffee. She handed me a cup and held hers as she sat on the edge of the bed. I sat down in a chair and she asked where I was from. I told her about Los Angeles and Newport Beach, Fresno and college. She listened to every word as she stared at me with those beautiful intense eyes so full of feeling. It was pain and warmth, tragedy and kindness all blended together that created a woman with a very deep soul. She finally said, "Why don't you just stay here with me, for the night?"

I looked at her surprised for a moment then realized this was business. "I don't have any more money."

She thought for a moment then said, "come back in two hours, I have to make a certain amount to pay for this room so if you come back you can stay and I don't have to charge you."

I was blown away. She wanted me to come back even though she knew I had no money. She wanted me for me. I could feel my confidence coming back, suddenly everything was different. She wasn't some heartless prostitute that just wanted my money; she was a woman who was interested in me. I smiled, "really?"

"Yes, come back, please...; promise you will."

I nodded, got up and walked toward the door; she walked with me, kissed me and I walked out into the night my mind roaring. Why would she do that? What did she have to gain? My own fragile self-esteem would not allow me to believe she would be interested in me for me there had to be a motive but what was it?

I walked the streets, my friends were not at the meeting place, but it was almost midnight, they were long gone. The bars were still jumping as I walked by, out of one; I could hear the Stones singing "Honky-tonk Woman", which somehow seemed appropriate.

I had no desire to go in and drink, I needed to think so I kept walking. Maybe I should just go back to the hotel, I thought, this is crazy. But I couldn't stop thinking about those eyes and that smile; no, I would go back, I had to see what would happen.

I walked for nearly two hours, along the canals the side streets and the main streets. This would be dangerous in most American cities but for some reason I felt safe in Amsterdam. It was the same beautiful city to me with the yellow streetlights that had dazzled me six weeks before. I loved Amsterdam. I loved Europe.

It was almost 2 am so I began walking toward Marta's apartment. I was getting nervous again although not as much as I had been before. I knocked on the door, she opened it and smiled. "You came back, I thought you wouldn't."

I walked in and sat on the chair, she said, "give me a moment" and she left the room.

As I sat there my thoughts began to arouse me. She wanted me, not just for the money. To me it made a difference. She was beautiful, experienced and older and she wanted me. When she returned, she was in a robe, she walked toward me, and I stood up and kissed her. She untied her robe and all that was under was her beautiful body. We made love, beautiful wonderful love and there was not one thought about her being anything but a woman who wanted to be with me.

After, we lay in bed and she told me about herself. She had a husband and two small children, twins. She had been married a few years when he had had a terrible auto accident that left him paralyzed and confined to a wheelchair. Because there was not enough money even with government disability, she decided to do this. She said it wasn't all that bad; the government controlled everything so it was a bit safer than it could have been. Of course, even though it was accepted in this country she was a social outcast to most of society. She didn't care; she had to take care of her family.

I never asked how old she was, I guessed about 30. I had the sense that she was a very brave and strong young woman. She didn't want to do this, sell her body, but she was willing to and made the most of it. She said her husband, sentenced to a life in a wheelchair, had become angry and mean. I could only imagine how awful it would be, knowing his wife had to do this to survive while he sat at home helpless. She didn't love him anymore, not because he was a paraplegic but because of whom he had become. But she couldn't leave him; he needed her, and she was taking that responsibility. I thought, he wasn't the only one sentenced for a lifetime, how would she escape this?

We talked for a long time, she was so easy to talk to, and in those small hours of the morning something happened between us, our souls met and I knew that I would be with this woman a long, long time, if I could. It didn't matter that she was married or that she was a prostitute, she was a beautiful woman outside and in. She had soul, more than any woman I had ever known. She was tender and caring and for that moment we were together, and the rest of the world did not matter. I fell asleep holding her in my arms.

I awoke at 7 and sat up. Jerry was probably worried about me; what was I doing? What was I thinking? I looked at Marta, she was asleep. As I moved to get up, she opened her eyes, "what are you doing, it's still early, go back to sleep."

"I have to go, my friend is going to be worried about me and I have to get ready, we're leaving today."

"Leaving, where?" She said. We had not talked about this.

"Home, California, this is the last day of our trip."

She stared at me and then tears came into her eyes. "You're going home to America?"

"Yes, I'm sorry I didn't tell you; I didn't think it mattered." I said.

"I thought you would stay, here in Amsterdam. We could be lovers; we could spend more time together. You could work and be with me. I don't want you to go."

"I don't either, but I have to, I have school and my family; they would never understand." I was trying to convince myself as much as her.

She stared at me, then got up, she was angry. "Why? I meet someone who is kind, who is different and now you are leaving?" She shouted to me and probably to fate.

"I'm sorry", I said. I got up and began getting dressed.

"No, wait, don't go yet. I will make us something to eat."

I was torn, my old enemy, should, was urging me to go but my heart said stay. She came up and put her arms around me and kissed me. We fell back in bed and made love again.

We laid there for a while and then I said, "I do have to go."

She looked away, "Ok", she said and got up. "You don't want breakfast?"

"No, I need to go." I said.

She looked at me with sad, haunting eyes; I felt terrible. How could I hurt this woman, it was crazy, we just met. But in those few short hours something did happen between us that was more than physical, and now I was walking away from it and we were both hurting.

"I will drive you to your hotel" she said.

We got dressed and walked out to her car. The morning was bright and beautiful, but I couldn't appreciate it. As she drove to the hotel, we said very little. I tried to make conversation, but she wasn't interested. She was closing me out. Just one more disappointment, one more hurt. She was probably used to them in a life that had given her beauty and a kind heart but a proportionate amount of tragedy and setbacks.

I wanted to scream, "Stop, I won't go, I'll stay with you", because at that moment there was nothing I wanted more. But once again, duty would win out over desire. She drove up to the hotel and I got out and walked around to her side of the car.

"Marta, I'm sorry. I will come back. I will finish school this year and come back."

She smiled; a sad knowing smile that said, it's a nice thought but I don't believe it. I bent down and kissed her, she grabbed my hand and held it as she sat in the car not saying anything. Then she let go and said "goodbye," and drove away, out of my life, forever.

I stood staring at the empty street. This is where it had begun. So much had happened and now it was over. My heart was aching. I didn't want to go. I loved it here, why was I leaving? I could stay, I could be with Marta, she could help me get a job and I would save money; go to Spain next spring. Why was I going home? To what? School? I hated school. My world? My world didn't work for me. Here was the most beautiful woman I had ever known who wanted me, appreciated me for who I was. I could love her; learn from her, I wanted to cry. Maybe it was the lack of sleep, the emotions of the trip being over or maybe it was how sad Marta looked, that last look, but I wanted to sit down on the curb and cry my heart out.

Instead, I rang the bell; Jerry had our only key. The door buzzed and I pushed the door in. As I walked up the stairs Lotte gave me a look, like any mother who would not approve of an older child's behavior but couldn't say anything. Back to reality, I thought. I found Jerry in bed still sleeping. I could see he was really worried about me. As I walked in, he woke up.

"Hay, where've you been?" he said.

I started to explain, but somehow, I knew the story would only come off as some superficial conquest and that the real substance of what I had just experienced would be lost on him. So, I glossed over it and asked how he and the Texans had made out. He told me that they had all found girls right away and told me about this beautiful young girl that he was with. They had waited for me for a while but finally figured I had already left so he came back to the hotel.

We ate our last breakfast; the ladies didn't say anything about me not being there, they knew it was not their business although I'm sure the urge to mother us was there. We took our time packing and then took a cab to the bus that would take us to the airport. We were at the airport a long time waiting. I read my book but had a hard time concentrating. I was tired but more than that I was very sad. The experience with Marta had touched me to the core and it just compounded my misery.

On the flight home I thought about all the people we had met. I would never see most of them again. Jerry and I would eventually drift apart, and it would only be me. All this part of my life was gone forever, and I didn't want it to be. The decision to return was a mistake, I know that now. I have few regrets in my life, but this will always be one of the big ones. I moved on to circumstances that conflicted with my soul and I would suffer the consequences. A disastrous relationship, dropping out of school in my last year and losing myself completely were those consequences. It didn't have to be that way. If I could choose again, I never would have left but it would be many years before I would discover that I could make choices no matter how radical and I could be free to follow my heart.

What I did not know at the time, was there were still adventures ahead of me and that I would return to Europe to attempt to find that lost vision and Marta. Still, that would be an entirely different experience. For the moment, I could only feel the end of an amazing adventure. Joe Turner was right; going to Europe, changed my life.

Many years later, I wrote these words: *There is a place in time that I would love to return. A place where Jerry and Sean, Mac and Stephanie, Anne, Bret and, of course, Marta are still in my life. Where Garmisch and Sitges, Amsterdam and Stockholm are all there and I can relive the experience, the people and the places.*

But of course, time brings changes. Changes in us, in the world we live and changes in the people who we meet and know and love. The children grow up and leave, the lovers don't belong together anymore and separate their lives; our grandparents and parents grow old and they leave too. We travel our life's path alone, but we are touched by them all. We are touched by our experiences and somewhere in time it is all still there, they are still there even though we don't see them anymore, they are there. The people we have loved, and the experiences are all there in our minds and our hearts and will remain forever in the recesses of our souls. And as our souls never die so too the people and experiences in time that touched our lives will never die.

BOOK II

THE GAP 1969 – 1971

Chapter 12

OUR LIVES ARE often defined by circumstances. Historical decisions, large or small, in world events, can change the course of our life that lie far beyond our own control. The decision to escalate the war in Viet Nam over the past four years, with no end in sight, was affecting lives in my generation, as well as their families, and would be the trademark of this era. I began my next year at Long Beach State, shortly after returning from Europe. Truly, my heart was not into going back to school, especially after the adventure I had just experienced. My freedom to drop out, however, was curtailed by a war that I wanted no part of, and the reality was, leaving school would make me eligible for the draft.

In the fall of 1969, I found an apartment on the second floor above a garage and house on 27th street in Newport Beach. I had discovered this place from a friend of a friend who was looking for a roommate. His name was Jeff and like so many young people in Newport, he was working and going to school part time. We agreed to share the two-bedroom flat and for the first time, I was rooming with someone I did not know and really, never did, as our worlds seemed to be in two separate orbits. He had his friends and I had mine; he had a girlfriend and I did not. The only thing I remember about Jeff was that because he was not a serious student, he was eligible for the draft and one day toward the end of my first semester at Long Beach that year, he got his greetings from the U.S. Government. The one other thing I remember about Jeff was, he was into Karate. So, one night, shortly before he was to report for his physical with the Army, he invited his Karate buddies over with the intention of breaking his collar bone so he would not have to report.

This was a different time in the world of young people; not like it was when my dad went off to war in World War II. Vietnam was an unpopular war and many young people were either refusing induction, which caused them to go to jail, or they were going to Canada, which made them an ex-patriot with ensuing consequences of separating from their families. Jeff's plan was, in my mind, crazy as his friends gathered to drink themselves into being able to carry out the act. I went to my bedroom, closed the door, and attempted to study with the sound of rowdy drunk commotion in the living room. I finally went to bed but before I could sleep, I heard the sound of a loud war cry whoop and then a painful scream; I assumed from Jeff. He actually did it.

As the year 1969 was ending, another Congressional event occurred that would change my life. On December 2nd of that year, a lottery was to take place to determine the fate of those individuals eligible for the draft. It was to be set by the person's birthday so 366 numbers were drawn and as they were, a numerical order was established. The smaller the number, the higher the probability was of being drafted. If the number was high enough, say after 200, you were likely not to be called. This, of course, was very interesting to me since I was in my fifth year of college and suspected my student deferment was now probably gone.

On the morning after the drawing I woke and immediately stepped outside, and down the stairs to the 27th Street sidewalk snatching up my copy of the Los Angeles Times. Standing on the sidewalk, I unrolled the paper, opened to the section with all the birthdays listed from the drawing, my heart beating in fear and anticipation and found my birthday – July 9th; it was 277. Smiling, I looked again to be sure I had read it right; running my finger across the row and realized at that moment, I would never be drafted.

My school year while living on 27th Street was filled with several groups of friends. There was the Newport Group and the Fresno Group, who often visited because I lived by the beach; a paradise compared to living in Fresno. Tom Spencer was my best Newport Beach friend who would become a life-long friend. I had met him while living in Costa Mesa in the summer of 1968; he was charismatic and down to earth, and we could discuss life as easily as we could discuss the pursuit of our fortunes and women. I became close with his family as well as his friends.

My connection to the Fresno friends came from my friendship with John Martin and Kenny Wilson, whom I had met while on the diving team in high school. Through them I got to know several people over my two summers in Newport when they came down during holidays and summer vacation. Of the individuals I became friends with, the Mitchel's had the most impact on my life. The family lived near where I did while in high school with a tyrannical father, 3 brothers and a very pretty sister, Sarah, who I attempted to date but for all the reasons why I was not dating at that time with anyone, it never happened with her either. Still, her brother, Steve became a friend and both he and Sarah talked often about their older brother Brian, who had been in the Air Force stationed in England. Prior to the summer of 1969, Brian was discharged and came back to Fresno, got married and tried to settle down. It didn't take and soon he was joining the rest of the Fresno group in parties and get-togethers that winter.

Brian and I bonded immediately. He was two years older; a natural leader who had accumulated many more experiences than I had up to this point in my life. But we had a common bond; Europe and a spirit for adventure, willing to risk security for the opportunity of having a more interesting life. It was only natural that when Jeff informed me, he would be moving out in the New Year that Brian would move to Newport and share the apartment with me.

1970 found me beginning my last semester at Long Beach State. I had been struggling with school mainly, I believe, because I did not like school, I never had. At this point, after continuous school for 17 years, I just couldn't devote the attention needed or the interest that would help me to be a good student. It became forced discipline that kept me going after I had been relieved of the concern of being drafted. I was not going to graduate in the spring, even though it was my 5th year of college. That, of course, troubled me deeply because it had been a life-long goal, mostly of my mother, to have a college degree. I was conflicted about not having a girlfriend since I broke up with Stacy Newman nearly a year before and finally, I was struggling with money, or the lack of money.

This time in my life was a sharp contrast to the freedom and joy I had recently enjoyed in Europe. As I look back at the beginning of 1970, I realize the impact of concern must have settled deep into my subconscious forever. Years after I graduated from college and married, I still continue to have recurring dreams of not graduating and of not having a woman in my life. All I knew at the time was I wanted to escape from the yoke of school, get a job, any job, and share my life with someone to love. Unknown to me, the wheels of fate were turning, and I was about to fulfill my desires that would change the direction of my life; some for better and some for worse.

Chapter 13

IT WAS BRIAN who came up with the idea. He had heard that Lake Tahoe was the place to go in the summer of 1970. There were plenty of jobs and it was beautiful country; a perfect place to re-locate. "Newport is nice, but I like the mountains. I read that there is a shortage of construction workers. I have been talking to Steve and we thought we should spend the summer there," he said.

Brian and I had formed a good friendship over the second semester of college and talked often of new adventures. One was saving money to go back to Europe, possibly buying motorcycles in England and traveling the continent like "Easy Rider". This new idea of going to Lake Tahoe, I had to admit, was intriguing.

"Have you guys decided when you would go?"

"We want to wait for Spring. It gets really cold this time of year. Maybe April or early May. You think you would want to go?" Brian said.

"Sounds good, but I need to finish the semester which will probably be the end of May," I answered.

So, about a month before my semester ended, Brian left with his brother Steve for Tahoe. I still had finals and my plan was to finish them and then follow the boys when I was done. I had one more item weighing on my mind that needed attention; paying a fine for a ticket I received for pulling in front of a car on Pacific Coast Highway after having dinner with some friends. Unfortunately, the car I pulled in front of was a Newport Beach Police Vehicle and he was only too happy to write me up. The ticket was to be paid a couple of weeks after Brian left, so I went to traffic court to ask for an extension. My thinking was I could get to Tahoe, make some money and mail the fine to the court. The Newport and Costa Mesa police and courts were extremely tough and showed no quarter, especially if you were young and happen to wear your hair long. My intention was to get a two to three week extension which would fall after I left for Tahoe. The judge gave me one week.

It was disappointing because I just did not have the money to pay the fine and I especially did not want to ask my parents or my Grandmother McKay who was giving me $50 a month while going to school. She was actually my step-grandmother and had graciously offered the money in honor of my grandfather, who she said would want to give it to me if he were still alive. I appreciated her kindness but dreaded seeing her each month at her house in Corona del Mar to pick up the check. Although she was kind, she was alcoholic and usually by the time I arrived, she was drunk, which changed her personality to very judgmental. I just did not want to deal with that another time. All I wanted to do was get out of town and decided I could make it. Once again, I underestimated Newport Beach law enforcement.

I had one final left and was studying at the breakfast table of my apartment in the morning, a day before the final when the doorbell rang. I figured it was one of my Newport friends stopping by to say good-bye, To my surprise, standing at the top of the stairs as I opened the door was a policeman who informed me I was under arrest for missing my extended court date. The judge had ordered a bench warrant when I did not show up in court. My plan to leave before I had to deal with this, was foolish optimism but in my most pessimistic thoughts, I certainly never expected to get arrested.

The police officer handcuffed me, escorted me to the car waiting in the street below and drove to the city jail just a mile from my apartment. I had never been to jail before, but I knew the drill from television; I could make a call after they processed me and took my mug shot. The person I wanted to reach was Tom but since there were only land lines at the time I could not reach him. I could not think of anyone else to call so I was taken to a 3 X 8 jail cell and left alone.

Morning turned to afternoon and I sat, bored and worried about not studying for my final. Finally, one of the police staff brought lunch and I asked to make another call. This was going to be a tough one because I knew I had to call my dad at work. Fortunately, my dad, who was always pretty cool, did not yell or make me feel bad; but he said he had no alternative but to call my step-grandmother, Clarice. "Oh my God, not that; I would rather stay in jail".

An hour later she arrived with her sister, paid the bail and I was released. As I expected, she immediately humiliated me with "how could you do this? Your grandfather would have been so ashamed that his grandson ended up in jail. Why didn't you call me if you needed money?" Because I knew it would be like this, I thought.

I managed to pass the last final the following day. As I walked down the hill from the campus to the parking lot, I let myself become excited about the adventure that lay ahead. What I did not realize was that it would be my last walk from the sprawling campus of Long Beach State. It would be 40 years until I returned for a visit with my daughter, Grace while shopping for colleges before she graduated from high school.

Chapter 14

BRIAN AND HIS brother Steve chose North Lake Tahoe since it was developing on that side of the lake. South Tahoe was the more popular tourist spot because of the Casino's but the north side of the lake offered more jobs for unskilled labor as well as cheaper housing. That summer not only did I follow the Mitchell's to Tahoe but many of my friends from both Newport and Fresno decided to migrate there, scattering along the 8 mile stretch of Highway 28 from Tahoe City to Kings Beach. Steve and Brian found a house in the hills above Carnelian Bay surrounded by twisting mountain roads and massive pine trees with houses and cabins nestled in between those trees on large irregular lots. They had two other guys living with them, but they assured me there was room for me to stay in an extra bed in one of the bedrooms. It seemed kind of crowded but for the summer I could handle just about any accommodation. As it turned out, it would be temporary because John Martin's parents owned a cabin overlooking the lake along Highway 28 near Dollar Point about 3 miles west of Mitchel's cabin.

I had assumed that Brian and Steve would have a job for me when I arrived but that did not happen; I was on my own. Since I had little money it was the most important objective of this new adventure. I began in Tahoe City going to restaurants and coffee shops looking for a dishwasher job but after several rejections I realized maybe this wasn't going to be as easy as I thought. Before getting too discouraged I walked into a small café nestled off the main roads of Tahoe City and asked an older man working behind the counter "do you have any jobs here?"

He looked me over for a moment then said "no but I have a customer who is managing a landscaping project on a new condominium project just a mile from here. He needs laborers."

He gave me directions to where Highway 28 met Highway 98 at the turn toward South Lake Tahoe and I left the shop with excited anticipation. When I arrived at the construction site, I saw brand new condominiums, some occupied but most empty, on a vast expanse of rocky terrain that surrounded the buildings. This is where the landscaping was taking place and where unknown to me, I would be working the next few weeks. I was hired by the foreman and sent to another location, the construction office, to process work related forms and told to be at the site at 7 am the next morning.

My job was raking the numerous rocks that covered the ground and digging trenches so that the irrigation lines that would be watering the future grass could be installed. I had worked in tough hard labor jobs in my young life; working in the farm fields south of Fresno, but this was some of the hardest work I had ever done. But when you are 22 the hard work that tore up my hands until they were bleeding and exhausted me to the point of collapse in the evening on the couch lasted only about a week as my body adapted to the work. I was a good worker and when the day came a month into the job, we were finished with that project, most of the labor crew was cut loose but I was one of two that was asked to move to another project in Incline Village, just south of the California-Nevada border on the Nevada side.

Over the past month I had moved out of Mitchel's cabin and took up quarters at John Martin's. Sarah Mitchell had followed her brothers to Tahoe and had talked John into letting her stay with us. It was a strange group of roommates with two bedrooms and a loft, where Sarah slept. I was still attracted to her, but she only wanted to be friends and so became more like a sister.

The new job in Incline was laying aggregate stones into freshly poured concrete on a huge driveway up and around the side of a monstrous home that sat on the edge of the lake. I was told that the home belonged to a Stouffer, of the Stouffer Food Company. He obviously had money because this was probably a second home. The work was tedious rather than hard and to break up the boredom I found myself talking trash with the other workers.

My usual routine while I worked in Incline for the month of July was to finish work, go to the cabin to change clothes then go back to State-line at Kings Beach to a bar called the Stop with John, Brian and the gang. We would mostly drink beer, sometimes with shots of Tequila and drive home intoxicated. Then I would wake at 6 a.m. the next morning, swearing I would not do that again and go to my job for another 8 hours of labor; then do it again that night to drink and look for the elusive summer romance.

One day, while working, one of the guys, an older surfer looking dude began bragging about what great shape he was in at 30. I was close to turning 23 with the summer nearly half over and felt I was in pretty good shape too after laboring for a few weeks. The talk flowed into who was stronger or better at various exploits and by quitting time at 4:30 p.m. we had challenged each other to a swim race on the lake from the back of the Stouffer House to a buoy about 50 yards out and back. Before we began, a couple of other guys joined in the race. I knew I could probably win because I was a good swimmer, but my older companion was pretty buff so it would be a good race.

The four of us walked into the cold water of Lake Tahoe and someone on the shore yelled go. I churned with all my might, determined to win, perhaps to help my damaged ego for not having a girl for the summer. By the time I got to the buoy, I was well ahead of the other three but my instinct at that point was not only to win but to slaughter them. Even after 8 hours of work and probably a drunken night before, I had the stamina to beat them all by 20 yards. It was a minor event, but for the rest of July I had a new self-esteem at work.

The summer of 1970 in Tahoe was filled with friendship as we listened to the music of Neil Young, Crosby, Stills and Nash and Chicago. The 4th of July was a special day that year. Brian and Steve set about filling ice chests with plenty of beer, sodas and food and we headed out early to find a spot at one of the many public beaches along the lake. It was on a Saturday that year, so we had all weekend to celebrate and celebrate we did. It was a day of swimming, drinking and just being young and in love with life, reminding me of the previous summer at Lake Eibsee in Garmisch. My Newport friends who were renting a single-wide in a trailer park in Tahoe City were there as well as Sarah and John from our Cabin. One of the Tahoe City boys, Terry Sullivan was a friend from Newport, and he was in Tahoe for a while with his brother, Gary from Paso Robles. Another arrival to the party that day was a very pretty friend of the group in Tahoe City that I had not met before. She smiled at me and not knowing who she was but attracted to her I walked over to where she was standing alone.

"Hi, I'm Andy," I said.

Her smile brightened as she responded, "hi, I'm Jennifer, but everyone calls me Jenny."

"I've never seen you here before, are you friends with Terry?"

"No," she said. "my boyfriend is a friend of his brother, and I came here with him."

"Who's your boyfriend?" I asked.

She motioned her head toward where Gary was standing and I noticed a tall nice-looking man, older than me talking with some of the boys. "That's Bart, but actually, we are not doing well."

"What do you mean?"

She looked out at the lake then back to me, "We've been together for a couple of years living in Sacramento, but I think the relationship has run its course. He doesn't know it; I'm going to break up after we go back. This was a bad idea for me to come; I think he thought we could put it together on this trip, but it isn't going well. He has more interest in his friends than me and the reality is, I just don't care."

I was surprised she was telling me all this, so open with her feelings even though we didn't know each other until this moment.

"What about you, who are you with?" she asked. "Let me guess; that tall blonde girl you were talking to earlier" she pointed to Sarah.

"No, we're friends. She is Brian's sister and I've known her for a couple of years. I think at one time we thought we could be more than that, but it just didn't take."

She watched Sarah for a moment then said, "so you're alone? What a waste."

I let out an embarrassed laugh feeling my face turning red but didn't say anything. Over the course of the day I continued to talk to her. She had striking features with raven black hair and large brown eyes. She was easy to talk to and it was nice for me to have some female company for a change. I didn't think I had a chance with her because she was still with her boyfriend and she was a couple of years older than me.

Late in the afternoon after most of us had enough sun, we moved the party to Brian's cabin. There was a large front yard, mostly dirt, but we moved some tables outside and fired up the barbeque and it was perfect for all the people who stayed into the evening. It was ideal for the Fourth because we were on a hill and could see fireworks being displayed from somewhere down by the lake. As the evening wore on, someone brought out a bottle of 151 Rum and poured shots. I had already discovered that summer that 151 was its own kind of drug that had to be consumed carefully. For me one shot was perfect to make you comfortable and mellow, 2 shots and you were on your way to being drunk and anymore and you were probably in trouble.

Most of the Tahoe City group including Jenny went back to their place. Terry Sullivan had chosen to stay with our group at Brian's and lost his ride back to Tahoe City. I volunteered to take him back after 2 shots and a long day of drinking. The two of us climbed into my car, a Plymouth Valiant convertible. I kept the top down most of the time and this night was no exception. It was a beautiful, clear night as we felt the air engulf us while I navigated a bit too fast around the curves of the mountain road that led to Hwy 28. Misjudging my speed, I swerved around a bend and launched the car off the road and down to a small meadow about 3 feet below. It was a miracle that we missed all the trees that we certainly could have, probably should have hit. The impact of the car hitting the ground jolted both Terry and I, but we were too drunk to feel any pain. That would come the next day. There seemed to be no damage to the car, and I managed to get it back on the road. Looking back now, I can't believe how stupid I was and how lucky. But stupidity is something young people do, and I was no exception.

Down the road from Cal/Neva, The California/Nevada border, a new casino was being built; a spectacular monstrosity on the North Shore of the lake that was to be called, Kings

Castle. Through the grapevine there was talk of a grand opening concert featuring B.B. King in Mid-July. I don't remember who decided to go, but I found myself in the car with some of the Tahoe City trailer guys and Jenny, sitting beside me in the backseat, heading for the grand opening. We probably had drinks before leaving because there was a lot of kidding and laughter as we made our way to the new Casino. Suddenly Jenny kissed my ear and whispered some provocative statement about what she would like to do with me. Me, the guy who never got the girl unless the girl chose me; and this woman, who still had a boyfriend, had chosen me.

We arrived at King's Castle to a crush of people also there to attend the opening. As our ragtag group moved through the crowd, I could see well dressed and glamorous people hovering around someone as if there had been an accident. Then I realized what the excitement was about; it was Bob Hope. I didn't even know he was going to be there. We continued moving to the ticketing in front of the theater where B.B. King was to play and eventually found our seats.

B.B. King was a rock and jazz guitarist that had risen to fame from the hit "The Thrill is Gone". Besides the one song, I didn't know too many others that he played, but his style was smooth, and my thrill was getting to see him play in person. My other thrill was sitting next to Jenny who whispered in my ear, "let's find some place to be alone after the concert."

I looked at her, smiled and nodded. I'm not sure how we managed to break away from the others after the concert; I believe they dropped us off at John's cabin where my car was parked after we made some excuse of hanging out there for a while. Instead we got into my car and found a motel near the state line and checked in. Jenny was a passionate and experienced lover and I had the same sensation I had with Marta the previous summer. I had been chosen by an older woman who was my superior in the art of love making and I just went along with the process.

By the time we left the Motel, it was 2 a.m. I drove her to the trailer park and our conversation centered on her going back to Sacramento. She was going to break up with Bart, she told me. He was going to find another place to live after he came back from Tahoe and she suggested that I might come see her before the end of summer vacation. She gave me her home phone number and told me "I will teach you more."

By late August the end of summer was near and so was my job at the Stouffer House. I had decided not to go back to school but instead take some time off in Fresno and Newport Beach before coming back to Tahoe to look for winter work at one of the many ski resorts that surrounded the area. I could not stop thinking of Jenny and resolved that during my time off, I would go see her in Sacrament. I had also been communicating with my old flame, Stacy Newman who was still in Newport. I had not seen her since I had left for

Europe the previous year, but we had recently talked by phone. It made sense for me to see her while I was in Newport and I told her I would call.

So here I was after going nearly a year without anyone, now making plans to see two women. I left Tahoe a happy man, planning this vacation in Southern California. I had money in my pocket, was not going back to school and had great plans before coming back to Tahoe for the winter. I decided to call Jenny on my way back to Tahoe. Driving down Hwy 99 toward Fresno I smiled to myself; life had finally come together, and I was feeling good about myself. I had no idea that it was really all about to crash in on me.

Chapter 15

STACY NEWMAN WAS my first experience of falling in love. We met in my senior year of high school at a party after a Christmas formal that I was invited to by Jeannie Edwards. It was called a girl's date because it was tradition for the girl to invite the boy. The party after the dance was at Jeannie's house and it was a small group made up of mostly the smart kids - advanced placement, which I never came close to being. Still, I was a senior and most of Jeannie's friends were juniors, including her, so I was able to fit in somehow. I remember how captivated I was when I met Stacy; she was pretty, smart and had a very sharp wit that was quite clever. I made up my mind that evening that I had to get to know her.

Over the Christmas vacation, I could not get her out of my mind. I wanted to call her but as always was nervous to make such a bold move. I learned from the party that she lived with her parents on Spring Street and so I looked up the number in the phone book and found her father's name, Edward Newman. That must be the one, I thought. But should I call her? Jeanie still liked me, but I was not interested in her. Stacy was with a guy named Wayne Harper, but were they an item or just friends? They seemed to be just friends but…I continued to torment myself with indecision. So, I decided to wait until school was back in session.

I had never seen her at school before but now that she was on my radar, I began to see her in the cafeteria at lunch time. My crowd at the time was dubbed, "the surfers" because we wore mostly blue jeans and t-shirts. Her crowd was the smart kids, HAP as we called them, an acronym for higher aptitude placement. I was definitely out of my league and moving into a new frontier. Still, I had to get to know her, she was all I could think of, but each time I thought of calling her my stomach churned. This was to be a trademark of my personality; shy when it came to potential rejection, but it was also an early lesson. Was the reward worth the risk? In this case I concluded that it was.

One evening, I finally found the nerve to make the call. Her father answered, which of course made my heart jump as I nervously asked to speak to her. "Hello", she said in that raspy but sexy voice that was her trademark.

"Stacy? This is Andy…McKay. We met at Jeannie's house after the Christmas Dance."

"Oh yes, that was a fun evening".

"It was, and I was glad I got to meet you." *Too bold, Andy, tone it down a bit. Take out*

"Me too", she responded. "I can't believe we never met before".

"I know." *Good, she was easy to talk too.* I continued, "So I was wondering if you would like to go to a movie this coming Friday or Saturday night?"

There was a pause, a hesitation; *she doesn't want to and can't think of a way out.*

Finally, "I thought you and Jeannie were going out".

"No, just that one date; she asked me".

"Oh, well I think she really likes you. If I go out with you, she is going to be mad at me."

My heart sank. "So, you don't want to go out with me?"

"Yes, I do, I just don't want to hurt her." She said. "Let me talk to her tomorrow and then call me back tomorrow after school"

As I hung up, I felt both relief and hope. *At least she wanted to go out, there was a chance.*

As it turned out, Jeannie was not happy. I was not a good guy as far as she was concerned and Stacy also was not winning any support; but against the tide, when I called her back that evening, she said yes. And so, began a nearly five year romance. Some of it was the kind of love that I have rarely experienced in my life; the kind that is usually only reserved for the young. Some of it brought devastating lows as we broke up and then went back together many times over those five years. Later, after she had gone away to college at Stephens, her very good friend, whom she had met there, told her that we would probably marry some day because we always came back to each other. Our final break-up was the previous summer shortly before I left for Europe.

Now, as I drove home from Tahoe, I thought about her and looked forward to seeing her again. I would discover later that she also was anticipating our meeting; more than I even knew.

Decisions in life are born from the forks we meet on the road of our journey. We can make good decisions but often our youth leads us to bad decisions made through our inexperience and impetuousness. I arrived in Fresno with the idea of staying at my parent's house for a few days before heading to Newport to see Stacy. I had no time itinerary and she was waiting for me to call before I came to see her. Life at home for a few days would be nice; it was always good to talk to my mother, who was a kindred spirit with me as opposed to my dad who did not like to talk deep but was a great friend to watch a game on TV or play golf. As I settled in, catching up on the adventures I could talk about, my mom mentioned her friend, Carole Bradford. She was a young lady she had worked with at one time who stayed in touch with mom. I had met Carole a few times when visiting from college, and one time she and my Sister Becky came down for a visit to Newport.

"She is a nice girl and a lot of fun. She recently broke up with her boyfriend; you should ask her out", mom said.

I recalled Carole did have a great personality, was kind of cute, not pretty and was a year older than me. I thought that as long as I was on a roll now with women that I should ask her out. Mom made it easy for me; she invited her to dinner at the house the very next evening. It was odd, actually, to be thinking of dating her. I never considered her date worthy, probably because she was my mother's friend. So, as I considered the possibility, I began to look forward to seeing her.

She had changed since I saw her last. Her brunette beehive hairdo that she had previously worn was now a Jane Fonda shag that was very cool at the time. She seemed younger and more attractive than I remembered. We had a nice evening with drinks and cigarettes at the bar, where my parents entertained before sitting down in the dining room for dinner. Carole was enchanting as her clever personality brighten the meal with my family. I watched her thinking, yes, I would like to spend more time with her.

Later in the evening, my parents went to bed and Carole and I stayed up talking. She told me she had seen my photos from Europe and was immediately attracted to me. She had wanted to see me but because of being friends with my mom she had not really considered it. It was funny, she said, that it was Liz's (as she called her) idea. We continued talking until late into the night. I told her of my plans to go to Newport, but before I left, maybe we could spend some time together. We made plans before she left for the evening to go out the next night.

Over the next two days we became inseparable. I discovered she liked marijuana, so we smoked pot together, which really made me laugh at the irony of my mother's friend being that cool. We spent time with my sister, who was also friends with Carole and the rest of the family and then we spent time alone. The more time I spent with her the more, I liked her. Finally, I suggested that she go with me to Newport. I decided I would have to postpone my call to Stacy; I wanted to spend more time with Carole.

I can't even recall what we did in Newport. Most likely we visited with my friend Tom, who was one of the few friends not in Tahoe that summer. He was now living in Costa Mesa. There were three little apartments behind a house and most of the occupants were friends of Tom. The apartment behind his small studio belonged to one of the guys who was still in Tahoe and Tom offered it to us for the night. Sleeping together for the first time was not particularly memorable. I remember more the fact that I was totally consumed by her personality and thought I was falling in love. As I look back now, I know it was not love but more of an infatuation created from being with someone who seemed to have fallen in love with me. Carole made me happy; gave me a feeling of having a woman in my life that I had missed over the past year. So out of the blue the morning after our first overnight together when she said, "I think we should be married", I actually thought it was a good idea. And so, began a two-month odyssey that took me literally to my knees.

It is easy today to look back and realize how stupid I was; but being in the moment all I knew was that I loved being with her and visualized a life of happily ever after; fairytale stuff from a dreamer who just had not had enough experience with relationships. We planned a wedding in her parent's backyard in Fresno. I called Brian to come down and be my best man and he agreed, although he thought I had lost my mind, which of course he was right. My dad took me aside and said that my mother was disappointed that we made these plans without talking to her. My mother told me confidentially how disappointed my father was for doing this so rashly. There were so many times after the invitations were sent that my inner voice told me to run, you are making a big mistake. Our friendship began to get a bit frayed as we got to know each other better but neither of us had the presence to realize we were making a mistake. I think we were both stuck in the fairytale dream and didn't want to let it go.

I called Jenny in Sacrament to let her know that I would not be coming to see her. I told her I had met someone but refrained from giving details of a pending wedding. The hard call was to Stacy. While I did not know of the extent of her desire to see me and perhaps resurrect one more time our relationship, I did know she would be disappointed. She did not take it well as I explained in more detail than I had with Jenny that Carole was an old friend and something magical had happened and we just decided to get married. Her response was, "I just can't believe it," over and over as if she were in shock, which actually she was. It was later that I found out that over the past year after we broke up, that she had been holding on to hope that we would be together again. That night, after our conversation she came close to suicide, had a major anxiety attack and had to be taken to emergency by ambulance. I just did not see that coming.

Carole and I decided we would move to Long Beach after the wedding and while waiting found a very nice one bedroom in Belmont Shores, an older well maintained and popular beach community. I began searching for jobs in the local paper and interviewed with a Life Insurance Company that sold policies door to door. I was told I needed to be licensed but they would put me through the training while paying me a minimum wage. Carole was pretty sure she could get a job at a bank since she had years of experience. The apartment was furnished and affordable because it was a beach summer rental and we were taking it in September. Our fairy tale was coming together.

It did not take long, after the wedding, for the wheels to fall off. The wedding was a nice party, not much more. Our two-night honeymoon at a local hotel was not the happy romp I expected. I was discovering that she did not really like sex; something I should have discovered sooner but didn't. Suddenly she was not that interested in spending time with me, but rather wanted to hang out with her family. Still, we managed to load up the wedding presents and some of her furniture in a trailer and move to our new apartment. We lasted a week.

I began my new job at the Insurance Company and discovered there was no way I was going to do what they wanted me to do. Carole critical of things that used to be ok and came up with excuses not to have sex. Day by day my self-esteem slipped as I realized I had made a huge mistake. One evening she announced that her family was taking their ski boat to Millerton Lake, one of the many lakes that are sprinkled in the California Sierra Mountains. They had rented a houseboat and several friends of the family had been invited to attend this annual trek. Carole decided she wanted to go for a couple of days early and since I was working could follow up on the weekend. I reluctantly agreed thinking this was not how I visualized our fairytale was going to evolve.

Carole ended up going to the lake ahead of her parents with some of the family friends. I arrived at her parent's house early Saturday morning and rode with them to Millerton. I recall it was not a pleasant ride; they were concerned about the behavior of their daughter and I was pretty upset myself. As it turned out when we arrived, Carole kept her distance from me, spending more time with her friends and I felt like some pariah who was a stranger to the whole clan. By Sunday morning I made up my mind I was going to leave the lake by walking to the main road and hitchhiking back to Fresno. I had to get out of there anyway I could. I told her father what I was going to do, and he talked me into waiting; they were going to leave later in the day and would take me back. It was one of the longest days of my life as I tried to fight back the anxiety that was gnawing at me.

Finally, it was time to leave. I told Carole I was going to drive back to Long Beach, rent a trailer and load all the wedding presents and furniture that belonged to her and drop everything off at her parent's house. In my pain, all I could think of was getting out of this madness. I did not want any of the presents I only wanted to go back to Tahoe. As I spoke to her, she only stared at me not saying a word. She was probably happy but had the good sense not to show it. As I climbed into her father's car, I had no idea that I would see her only one more time, when I dropped the furniture and presents off at her parent's house.

I drove back to our apartment at Belmont Shores, my heart aching as I looked at the many wedding presents, some still in their boxes and Carole's furniture that had been there for only a week. I called Tom to see if he could come up and help me load the U-Haul trailer I had rented. He did not hesitate, and his presence was more than just helping load the trailer; his friendship and understanding was what I needed most. As the song said that was written years later by Burt Bacharach and Carole Bayer Seger; *That's What Friends Are For.*

Chapter 16

I HAVE DISCOVERED over the years that life is such an interesting journey. We flow in and out of good and bad times and in each of these we feel it will never end. Mercifully the bad times make way for the good and the pain that goes with any loss dissipates to just a memory; although the soul, it seems, is scarred for life. Fortunately, the pain gets buried in the subconscious and only comes back to haunt us in our dreams. For the next two months I grieved over the loss of what I believed was to be the fairytale relationship. I also felt the pain of embarrassment for letting myself get into such a mess. My friends were great but after a while no one wanted to be around someone who was in deep depression. I ran out of money in Tahoe and could not find a job. My plan of finding work in one of the ski resorts was hampered by the fact that there was not an early snow that year. Finally, I had to leave the mountain and go back to Fresno. The whole experience back to Tahoe was a humiliating contrast to the summer that had held so much joy and promise.

Finally, free from going to school I learned that I was now in the world of having to work and earn enough money to be independent. The harsh fact was, I needed to live with my parents until I could find my way back to the freedom of independence while carrying the weight of a broken self-esteem. The question was what kind of job I could find with no real skills or experience and no degree. Brian came down from Tahoe the same time I did as his job situation in Tahoe was over. He still had money but knew it would run out soon, so he made plans to work with his father who was now living in Valencia. Steve was still working and would be one of the few who would remain in Tahoe for the winter.

It was just a couple of weeks after we left the mountain that Brian called and told me, a friend of their family, David and Louise Becker owned a flower shop downtown and needed a part-time delivery person. They had someone working the afternoon shift but needed coverage for the morning hours. I met them and was hired immediately, mostly because of my friendship with the Mitchel's. Mr. Becker was a cantankerous and sarcastic boss that was hard to make happy. Mrs. Becker was like a sweet elderly grandmother that continually told me I needed to go back to school. The job was from 8 a.m. to noon and the main purpose of me being there was to deliver flowers in an old white van that was outfitted with a large box with divided sections that allowed flower arrangements in vases to ride without tipping over. Other than delivery, which wasn't very much, Mr. Becker wanted me to keep busy. So, every day, I swept the sidewalk, cleaned all the glass counters and the big refrigerator glass container that housed the flowers. Usually I had to look for things to do but always looked forward to doing the deliveries.

The fall months gave way to winter and I continued my morning job and looked for another job in the afternoon. But there just wasn't anything that I could do. I found that the flower shop survived on seasons and funerals. There were life-long customers of the Becker's that ordered birthday and anniversary bouquets to homes and businesses, but the only holidays were Thanksgiving and Christmas in the last two months of 1970. During that time as winter set in and it became cold in Fresno, the fog became a problem. It was bad enough during the morning hours but at night it was almost impossible to navigate through the town.

Mr. Becker planned on me working full time during the week before Christmas because he got so busy dispatching Poinsettia's and Christmas bouquets that he needed a second driver in the afternoon. Finally, on the day before Christmas, I found myself working into the night that Christmas Eve. I recall very clearly driving through the fog trying to find streets with a map and house numbers that were extremely hard to see in the foggy darkness. I had the radio on and listened to non-stop Christmas songs including the one I loved the most and still do; "Have Yourself a Merry Little Christmas". I was finally over Carole. I had filed for an annulment on the grounds of not consummating the marriage while I was back in Tahoe and it was granted. So, on this evening I had a wonderful sense of well-being. It was Christmas and Christmases at the McKay household were always special. It would begin with friends of my parents coming over for "high balls" and smoking cigarettes. There would be a party I was sure at the house when I got home from work and the next day, Christmas, would be full of all the Southern California relatives drinking, eating and opening gifts.

I had a feeling that as 1970 came to an end, the New Year would bring new adventure and opportunity. It was the optimism that I naturally had even after the devastating experience with Carole that allowed me to move out of my depression and look forward to better days. I would learn over the years, as I navigated many highs and lows of life, that the most important gift you can give to yourself is the gift of positive hope. There is always a solution to problems and negative circumstances, and by having that attitude you can and do rise above the challenges that life sometimes serves up.

Chapter 17

THE MOST MEMORABLE news event in 1971 was the "Pentagon Papers" which was the news leak from the New York Times and the Washington Post of government classified information over the reality that the Viet Nam War was considered un-winnable yet young men were continuing to be sent to fight and die in South-east Asia. A survey was released that indicated that over 60% of Americans were against the war.

As world events continued to unfold, my own world was about figuring out how I could get another job in order to save money so I could get back to Newport Beach. I did not have to wait long. In January, Mr. Becker told me his good friend Gill, who worked as a window dresser at the Coffee's Clothing store needed a part-time printer for the placards that advertised brand names of clothes displayed in the windows of their two Fresno locations. He had talked to Gill and said I was available to work in the afternoon. It was perfect; I had an 8-hour workday now, even if it was still only minimum wage which was $1.65 an hour that year.

My workshop was in the basement of the downtown Coffee's store which was just a few blocks from Becker's Flower Shop. Gill was an easygoing boss and the work was much more interesting than the flower shop, but the highlight of the job was Gill's assistant, who dressed the mannequins for the window displays, Vickie. I learned from her that we had been in 8th Grade together although I did not really remember her. Now, though, I could not forget her. She was tall, confident and beautiful and I fell for her almost immediately. I knew though, she was probably a heartbreaker and could easily crush mine, so I did not even consider being more than just a friend. She was out of my league.

I still needed to make more money and one day I saw in the classifieds of the Fresno Bee that H&R Block was looking for someone to be a math checker at night. The hours were from 6 p.m. to 9 p.m. and I figured that would round out my day nicely. Since I did not know what a math checker was, I just went in after my day at Coffee's and asked. I was told that each tax return had to be checked for math because in those days there were no computers and every return was done by hand. The lady who I interviewed with asked if I could work a 10-key adding machine. I said probably because I had worked with my dad's office a few times. So, she gave me a test and as I hunted and pecked each key she laughed and told me "you have to be faster than that; like this", as she demonstrated by rattling numbers and entries with her fingers flying over the keys without looking at them.

I left a bit humiliated but decided I would practice at my dad's office and learn to do what I needed to get that job. In just a few days I was back into the H&R Block Office demonstrating my new skills to the same lady. I think she was impressed and liked me for my tenacity. I met with the manager and was hired that evening, which began a brief career path that would follow me for several years. I was now making enough money to save so that I could eventually move back to the beach. I had asked Tom to be on the lookout for potential jobs and I set my mind to be able to move by the beginning of summer.

The call came in late March. Tax season was in full swing and I had earned the respect of all three employers because I had a good work ethic and was reliable; something I took for granted but was to discover, it was not that common with young people.

My mother handed me the phone, "for you", she said.

"Hello", I said into the receiver.

"Hi Mac", came Tom's familiar voice.

"Hi Pal, what's up?"

"I think I have a job for you". He went on to explain that there was a factory in Costa Mesa that made sporting goods equipment. He had a friend who worked as a fork-lift operator there and thought he could get me a job. The company was AMF Voit, a union job and the pay was in excess of four dollars an hour over double what I was making in Fresno.

I told him I was very interested and that I would finish my job at H&R Block on April 15th which would be a good time to leave the other jobs and move down. Tom was living in the small bungalow on Anaheim Street and said I could sleep on the couch that made into a bed for a while. The plan was in place and for the next couple of weeks; all I could think of was making my escape. I gave my notice to Mr. Becker and Gill for April 15th which was a Thursday. That day I said goodbye to the Becker's and to Gill and Vickie. Then I went to work for my last day at the tax office. I would discover that in the income tax preparation business, when the office closed at 9 p.m. the party began and so it was that year. I had more to celebrate than just finishing the tax season; I was about to launch a new adventure and I was thrilled. The following day, Friday, I packed my Plymouth Valliant Convertible; said goodbye to my family and set off for Newport. Although I had not secured my new job, I had the belief it would work out. I had a place to stay with Tom and had money; my world certainly looked brighter than it had six months before.

Chapter 18

TOM'S PLACE WAS small; perhaps the size of a single wide mobile home. The couch/ bed was in the room that was the size of a dining room; but he didn't need a dining room because he had a kitchen bar. The idea was for me to pay half the rent once I started the new job. I had been to Voit on Harbor Lane, just north-east of the 405 Freeway and met Tom's friend Mike. The place looked huge, but I only got as far as the front offices to fill out my application. Mike said they were constantly opening positions in the factory and since it was a union run company the openings were always offered to the current employees first. The jobs that would be available were the less attractive to current workers so he was sure something would open soon.

By the first of May I got a call on Tom's phone informing me a position had opened up. It was working the graveyard shift from 11 p.m. to 7 a.m. in the rubber press section of the factory. I was told to wear steel toed shoes and a long sleeve work shirt. It was the start of my year-long experience of working in a factory, which was a unique culture from any I had experienced before or after. Inside a monster building that was heavily guarded and gated for security reasons, was a small city of activity that continued 24 hours a day. Each section of the factory was responsible for some part of making sporting goods equipment. Footballs, basketballs, bowling balls, bowling pins and the section I was in; deep in the interior of the building almost to the furthest wall from the entrance was the section that made rubber equipment like swim-fins, masks, kicking tees and baseball home plates. In this section the temperature was at least ten to fifteen degrees hotter than the rest of the factory because of the hot presses lined up in three rows.

There were six men for each shift and each man was responsible for seven machines. The way it worked was to approach a machine just as it was opening, stick your arms into the oven without touching the walls or the molds which radiated intense heat; take an air gun and release the finished product from the mold; then replace raw rubber chunks on the empty mold, press the button and move to the next machine. Each machine was timed so that ideally you were in constant motion. There was a quota of finished products each man was expected to produce in his shift. We were given a 30-minute lunch break and two 15 minute breaks.

My biggest concern, as I began the job, was putting my arms in the hot press molds and understood why we were told to wear long sleeve shirts. One touch to your skin and your arm would be seared as if it had been touched with a branding iron. I wanted no part of that and for the first couple of weeks always had a long shirt on. But as the summer months began and I became used to the balance of working these machines I gradually began working in short sleeved t-shirts with the same swagger as all the other press operators. Did I every burn myself? Almost every night but I got used to it and although I carried burn scars on my arms for several years, it was just part of the job. The pay was good and the work tolerable and soon I had decided that I would save my money and go back to Europe within a year.

Our union was the United Rubber Workers, a division of the AFLCIO and like all companies there was a hierarchy within the factory. The individuals who had the most seniority, not only made more money and got better jobs, but were the top dogs of the factory workers. Even some of the guys in my section who worked the day shift, showed up early wearing nice clothes and changed before beginning their shift which I found very strange until I found out they did it to impress their neighbors and family to believe they had better white collar jobs. Some of the guys on my shift were my age, 23, married with kids and had no way of getting out of working in the factory with a family to support. They were unskilled and un-educated so where else could they go and make the kind of money they were making? I often wondered about them when the plant shut down a few years later. Where did they go?

My foreman's name was Earl, a lifer in the plant. He seemed old but was probably in his fifties. His job was to supervise press operators and make sure we kept up with our quotas. He was a good guy but seemed dead inside as if all ambition and joy had been slowly sucked out of him over years of working in a dead-end career. As for me, I was thrilled to have a good paying job but had no intention of staying for more than a year. I was happy to be an independent adult; free to enjoy the coming summer months in Newport Beach only responsible for myself.

While I was living with Tom on Anaheim Street, I met a lady named Tammy, who was probably my age but looked older I surmised because she took uppers, which we called speed. She was wired tight and didn't sleep at night. She would have been perfect for me while I worked the graveyard shift, but I was only with her before the job started shortly after I arrived in Costa Mesa. She was like a stray cat that I met at a party in the front house, the first Saturday Night I arrived. I didn't know where she came from, but she was nice and we talked about life, one of my favorite subjects. She was married and her husband was in Viet Nam. She was lonely, high on drugs and before the night was over, we were back at Tom's place making love on my new bed. That was the end of the night for me as I fell into a blissful semi-alcoholic sleep. For her, she remained awake for hours, finally slipping into bed with me as the first light of day dawned.

Our affair was not long. She came around at night; I never knew where she went when I wasn't with her and really didn't care. Still every few days she would show up. We would drink, talk then go to bed and then she would leave. Sometimes she would stay all night, but rarely did she ever sleep. One morning I woke and saw her sitting in a chair staring at the window. I wondered what she was thinking. Who was this crazy girl? I liked her but I knew we would never be together for any length of time. After my experience with Carole, I just wasn't interested in getting involved with anyone. My desire to have a girlfriend was gone.

I got out of bed, dressed and decided to go to the local coffee shop on Harbor Boulevard. "Want to have breakfast?" I asked.

"I'll go with you", she said. "I'm not hungry but I can watch you eat".

So, we went and I appreciated her company; she probably appreciated mine. As I ate, I looked at this strange young lady; so thin, pretty but already declining and I felt for her but did not want a project. I was trying to put my own life together and certainly did not need her baggage. The bill came after I had finished eating and I pulled my wallet out to pay but realized there was money missing. Not a lot but I didn't have a lot. "That's funny, there's money missing. I know I had more than that".

"How do you know?" she said.

"I always know how much I have; it's too important to me at this point"; which was the case for many years of my life.

"Oh wow, you are something", she said. "Is it that important to you?"

I was becoming irritated with her, "yes, it is." She shifted and looked down like a child. "You took it didn't you?"

"No", she said unconvincingly.

There was a long silence then finally she reached in her pocket and pulled out a five-dollar bill and put it on the table. "Sorry, I didn't think you would miss it. I don't have any money."

I looked at her, angry and feeling sorry for her at the same time. "So, you went through my pockets while I was asleep?"

She nodded like a child in trouble and waiting for punishment.

Looking back, I would like to think I gave her the money back. I can't remember but based on my thinking at that time I probably kept it. We went back to Anaheim Street in silence. There was no yelling or fighting; it was just an impasse of, I didn't understand how she could do that to me, and I would never trust her again. For her it was, how could I be so petty over money. At the house she whispered something about leaving and walked out of my life as strangely as she had entered it. I saw her over the summer at various gatherings, but we never talked again. I am not proud of the way I treated her and can only use the excuse that I was still raw inside. I was over Carole, I thought, but the scars still showed.

Chapter 19

AS SUMMER APPROACHED, Tom came up with a great idea. "This place is too small for both of us. Why don't we try to get a house to live in while owners are away on vacation?"

"How are you going to do that?" I asked.

"We can put an ad in the Penny Saver advertising that we are professional house sitters. People do that all the time to watch the house, take care of their pets and plants."

We were sitting at the small bar off the kitchen having an evening drink where we often came up with ideas about women, life and what we planned to do with our lives. Tom was like a brother and together we had some wild dreams.

"Will, I guess it's worth a try", I said.

So, he placed the ad and we waited…but not for long. Tom got a call from a woman, Mrs. Thornton whose husband had recently died. She wanted to go to Pittsburgh to visit family but had two cats and did not know what to do; so, when she saw the ad, she thought it was a perfect solution. We went together to a very nice neighborhood close to Newport High School in Newport Heights to interview. She was planning on being gone a month and was not only concerned about her cats but also of leaving the house empty for that long. We told her we both had jobs and there would be no charge, since we would be saving on paying rent. She was a sweet lady and apparently, she trusted us; two somewhat clean-cut young men and so she agreed.

The house was a very clean three-bedroom, two bath and nicely furnished. She left in late June and we moved in for the whole month of July. I had plenty of friends who came by and we celebrated my 24th birthday at the house. As had been the case since breaking up with Stacy in the summer of 1969, I still had no woman in my life. I wanted someone but was just too shy and after Carole, I had no confidence. It had become a way of life that I was unfortunately getting used too.

My thoughts often went back to Vickie. I really liked her and although knew she was not interested in me, I thought of her as an ideal woman that I wished I could qualify to be with. One day I decided to write a note telling her I missed her and thanked her for the good time we had working together. In my short life I realized that I really did love women and that there were women that I liked, like Tammy but did not want to be with long term, and there were the untouchables; the ones you would fanaticize about but had no hope of attracting. I would learn later that beautiful women are confident in their looks are also insecure and many are damaged from love. It can range from frustrated anger to heartbreak and even though beautiful, they are not immune to love's challenges. In the summer of '71', I experienced both the one-night stands and a couple of untouchables; but mostly I was sleeping alone.

Toward the end of July, Tom and I had to look for a new place to live. We began by advertising again about house sitting and tagged ourselves now as "Experienced house-sitters." This time we had no takers and we were facing the reality of being homeless. Once again it was Tom who came up with the solution. "McKay, you know that room behind my parent's house on Cypress Street, why don't we stay there?"

I recalled his dad had built this little house and used it occasionally for parties and storage. It had seen better days and stood as a shell with broken windows, no insulation and no heat or cooling. There was no bathroom and what was most interesting was that in the back of the so called "house", was a neighbor's horse coral with several horses boarded. Think odor and flies. But when you are 24 and it is a free place to stay, I thought it was a great idea.

There were two beds, a couple of chairs and a couch, and we were able to fix it up to be pretty nice. Tom's mom, Betty, was thrilled to have us so close. There was a bathroom we could use off their kitchen so that really was no issue. So, after Mrs. Thornton came back from Pittsburgh, we moved into Cypress Street. Mrs. Thornton was happy with our house sitting; her cats and plants were still alive, and the house was intact.

Chapter 20

THE ONLY MAILING address I had was still on Anaheim Street. Tom spent time over at the front house visiting friends and would pick up any mail we had. One day he brought a letter from Vickie. To be sure it was the highlight of my day probably of my whole summer to hear back from her. She said she was so happy to hear from me, she also missed me and considered me especially thoughtful for writing. She went on to suggest that if I were in Fresno, she would love to see me again. That was the most beautiful music to my ears and my mind began to plan a trip to Fresno soon.

To say that Vickie was unique is a huge understatement. She was the girl who hung out with the bad guys, while I worked with her. She was not only pretty, she was tough in the way that no one was going to get into her heart or have any chance to break it. I was pretty sure that had happened in her past and that was why she was so guarded. She was a nice person; the kind that would help someone down on their luck, but she would take no shit from anyone. That is probably what attracted me to her, the challenge. I set a weekend in August to go to Fresno and see her.

I looked forward to our weekend together but was not sure what to expect. Did she expect me to stay at her house or just go out and I should stay at my parents? Unfortunately, I chose wrong and put myself in the middle of Vickie and my mother. My parents now lived on Olive on the north side of Fresno and I arrived in the late afternoon on Friday. My family was happy to see me; it was the first time I had been home since I left in May. My younger sister, Mary, was 16 and still in high school. Becky, my other sister was 21 and married, living also on the north side with her husband, Joe.

My intention was to spend the weekend with Vickie but when I showed up at home my mother's intention was that I was spending the week-end with them. This was one of the conflicts that I got myself into; not doing what I wanted but doing what I "should". I had this beautiful and mysterious young woman planning to be with me for the weekend and I had erroneously just assumed we were just going out on a date. I totally got my wires crossed.

I arrived at Vickie's house in the older downtown area of Fresno that Friday evening. She greeted me with a huge smile and as we hugged, she said, "Where are your clothes?"

"I stopped at my parents first. I wasn't sure if I was staying with you, so I left everything there."

Her smile faded, "oh, well, are you going to stay here?"

I recovered quickly; this was starting out badly. "Yes, of course I would rather stay here, I just wasn't sure that was what you planned. I will stay here."

She smiled again; a great full smile that lit up her face. "Good, it was probably my fault, we didn't really talk about it. I forgot your parents are here too. Want a Margareta?"

And so, our evening began. It was one of those magical evenings, the kind you think about in the emptiness of solitude when your fantasies of love from some movie make you long for such a night. We talked about our lives since we had seen each other over a few Margareta's, then went to dinner at a small café near her home. Eventually we made our way back to her bed, made love and fell asleep in each other's arms. I could not have dreamed of a better outcome, but I was conflicted.

Why had I told my mother I was in town? The answer was, I really did not think that Vickie would expect me to spend the weekend with her. I had no reason to believe it and I way underestimated her expectations. Now my mother would wonder why I had not come home after my date and worse yet, she wanted me to join the family at some celebration at my sister, Becky's house on Saturday. So, in the morning over coffee I explained the dilemma and asked if she would like to go to the party with me in the afternoon. She of course declined; she was not the kind of woman to go meet the parents at this point in our relationship and she had little sympathy for my situation. I knew I was losing points with her by opting to be with my family rather than her.

What to do? Looking back on it, I should of, probably would have told my mother what happened and stayed with Vickie. But at that time in my life I feared the wrath of her disappointment more that even losing face with Vickie. So, I took a chance that I could make it work. I went to the party which started later than planned, got stuck and had no way to call Vickie because I did not have her number with me and finally at seven made my escape still upsetting my mother for leaving early.

I arrived at Vickie's house wondering if she was upset with me. I rang the bell and waited. She opened the door and stood there looking at me. God she was beautiful; dressed in designer jeans a flowing top with her light brown hair falling over her shoulders. As I stood there, I somehow knew I was about to get kicked to the curb. This woman was strong and not about to suffer fools and, in her mind, I certainly qualified as one big fool. Suddenly she turned without a word and went back into the house. I followed her apologizing for being late and explaining I did not have her phone number. She walked into the bathroom and put some finishing touches to her makeup not responding to my apology.

"What are you doing" I said.

"Putting on my makeup", was her flat reply.

"Are you going somewhere?"

Silently without looking at me she picked up her bag and walked back toward the front door. Finally, she answered. "Yes".

"Where?"

"Out; I'm going to find some girls."

I was not sure what she meant by that; was she into women? I followed her out the door and she got into her car rolled the window down and looked at me very much the way Marta had looked at me from her car window in Amsterdam, that stoic and hurt look of disappointment. She did not say anything, and I couldn't think of an appropriate comment, so I stayed silent. I just stood there watching as she drove away. I never saw her again. One more person, that I truly cared about, out of my life forever.

Shortly before I left for Europe the following year, I was visiting an old friend, Jim Reeves. He had been living in Fresno and was much more connected to any gossip or news than I was. I mentioned Vickie and how I still felt bad for how that had gone down.

"I heard she had a baby," he said.

"Really, who is she with?"

"I don't think anybody."

"When did she have it?"

"I don't know."

I did the math; was it possible? It was possible. Was that her plan? I would never know but often wondered. It would be like her, whether planned or not, to raise a child alone, rather than let anyone be part of it. Perhaps there was more to our brief time together that weekend; or maybe that is just a fantasy. I do know that as I look back over my life, it has been the women more than anything else that has given it meaning. For whatever reason, I have a great love for them and a great longing to find lasting love. Most, though, have only been a season in my life, but those seasons are the pages of my life that have made it interesting and I can honestly say, I loved them all.

Chapter 21

THE SUMMER OF 71 was coming to an end. I still was living in the back house at Tom's parents, but now without Tom, who had talked about saving his money and going with me to Europe, but instead, decided to take a mini-van across the U.S. That left me alone in the house which was fine because his parents, Betty and Brick, were great hosts and refused to take any money while I stayed there. I often found myself in their kitchen; that seemed never to be without their friends, drinking, smoking, and laughing; very much as my parents did at that time. It was a different era; one that I miss.

I was still working nights at Voit and continued to save for the trip to Europe. I had made friends with the guys on my shift and developed a pattern of talking as we passed to and from each press, calculating the timing of our scheduled rounds. It was that social part of the job, mostly frowned on by the management that saved me from losing both my arms one night.

One of the presses I operated was a large two layered mold that made baseball home plates. The mold was held to the machine with four large bolts, one at each corner of a square shaped press and threaded through the layers of iron. As the press opened, it would separate into two parts: one above the other. As I approached that machine I would usually in order to save time, put my arms into the spaces as the press was opening, releasing the finished home plate with an air gun, then placing a black rubber chunk on the bottom and a white one on the top before sending the molds back together.

One night, as I was walking toward the home plate molds, I stopped to talk to one of the guys and was delayed in getting to the opening machine. Realizing the press was opening, I turned to see one final thrust of the separating molds when suddenly the top mold, which was probably 200 pounds, separated from the bolts and came crashing down on the lower mold. I stood frozen, as I realized that normally my arms would have been in that press and I surely would have crushed or severed my arms. At first, I was angry that the machine had not been maintained or the foreman did not see that those bolts were about to be sheared. Then the anger turned to gratitude that fate or God had delayed me that night.

Before 1971 ended, there were two events that would create a significant change in my life. My usual routine on Friday after my last shift of the week was to wake at around two in the afternoon and go to the bank to make my weekly deposit into a savings account. On the way, I notice a banner on one of the office buildings at the corner of Harbor and Newport, advertising "Income Tax Training." Because I had worked at H&R Block the previous tax season the banner caught my attention. It occurred to me that if the hours were right, I could take the class and make some extra money preparing tax returns. The timing would be good because my plan now, was to go to Europe in May. This might be a good way to add more money toward saving and an opportunity to learn something that could be helpful later, when I returned from Europe.

The class was 3 hours, from 7 pm to 10 pm which allowed me to attend once a week before going to work at Voit. Classes were to begin in October and would be complete by December. If I completed the course, the manager said he would hire me part time, working nights and weekends. It made sense to me, so I signed up.

My life soon became structured with work and tax classes. Tom was gone; I had a few friends but for the most part my life was lonely. I began reading James Michener's "The Drifter's", a story of young people like myself who meet by coincidence in Europe. It was the perfect book that I identified with as I dreamed of having the same adventures as the people depicted in that novel. I also spent quite a lot of time playing my guitar, writing songs and poetry, some of it was actually good, I thought. I discovered that being alone, which could be lonely was a good time for introspection and creativity. At 24, I had already realized that I loved to look at life and people and wondered why some seemed to enjoy their lives and some, quite the opposite, were unhappy. I read the popular book at the time, Maxwell Maltz, "Psycho-Cybernetics", which was a new revelation to me; that we could actually control our happiness by changing the way we looked at ourselves and our lives. It was a philosophy that even though far from perfected, carried me to the end of the year, enjoying my life and being excited, as I anticipated the coming New Year, which was to be filled with more promise and adventure than I even knew at the time.

As always, I was home for Christmas which was on a Saturday in 1971 and gave me two nights before returning to work, Christmas Eve and Christmas Day. In typical fashion, the house was filled with friends and family, mostly gathered around the bar my dad had built in the corner of the kitchen replacing the area designed for a breakfast nook. It did not matter whether there were four or fourteen people; there was always lively banter and intelligent conversation about politics and world events. My dad was a Republican, my strong-willed mother a Roosevelt Democrat so it was a great catalyst for exchange of contrasting ideas and opinions.

It was on this particular weekend that my dad asked about what I was doing with my life and of course the subject of, "was there any women in my life?"

I told him "no, not anyone special."

He continued, "Your mom and I were at a Christmas party a few days ago and saw Jack and Sheryl Zimmer. Sheryl told us that Christina had recently broken up with her boyfriend. You should give her a call; I think she is a cute girl."

I knew Christina because she had dated the son of my parent's best friends, Lee & Lois Carpenter. She was cute but she was six years younger than me and I had never considered her as someone I would ever date.

"That's not a bad idea; maybe I will call her." I said.

"Yeah, New Year's Eve might be a good time to go out with her."

I had to admit my dad had a good plan for me. I hoped it would turn out better than my mother's suggestion of taking out Carole. I also wondered what was wrong with me that I had to get dates from friends of my parents.

On Monday, following Christmas I made the call. Sheryl, her mother answered and seemed very happy that I called. Christina was taking classes at Fresno Junior College and Sheryl told me she was at school but to call back around five o'clock. When I did call back, Christina answered, anticipating my call. She was easy to talk to and we carried on a conversation for almost fifteen minutes about her world; school and her part-time job. I told her what I was doing; Voit, H&R Block and living in Newport Beach. Finally, I got around to asking if she was available to go out Friday night on New Year's Eve. Her answer was yes and did I have any particular plans. I had not even thought that far and replied that I did not.

"Well, my friend, Donna, who is married, is having a New Year's Eve party. Maybe we could go there." I agreed that would be fun and we set a time for me to pick her up.

On Friday, I picked her up in my Valliant and we went to Donna and Mick's, who had been married after Donna had become pregnant at 15 years old. Christina had remained her best friend through all of the turmoil and insult that goes with high school pregnancy. That was one of the things I liked about her; she was a loyal friend.

Most of the people at the party were Christina's age and at 24, I felt like the old guy. As the evening wore on, I got to know Christina more and found that I really liked her. We kissed at midnight, and I kissed her again at her door at the end of the evening. I told her I would like to see her again. It was the beginning of a New Year; one that I knew was going to be everything I had hoped for and more.

BOOK III

EUROPE 1972

Chapter 22

THE SETTING FOR the new year, 1972 looked promising. How good it was to be young, with so much life ahead; especially now that I possibly had a new girl in my life and it was only four months before I was to set off on my adventure to Europe. By contrast, the world as always was embroiled in tension and of course the media, which consisted of radio, television and newspapers, made sure we were aware of the daily dysfunction. This was the year that our President, Richard Nixon, would become embroiled in what would be known as Watergate. That, of course, was not to be revealed while the election year was in progress and even though most young people were against the Viet Nam War, there were not enough votes to carry the anti-war candidate, George McGovern to victory. This was also the summer of the Olympics that were to be held, in Munich, coincidently at the same time I intended to be in Europe. It would become one of the great tragedies of Olympic History.

I continued working at Voit, saving money, and focusing on my plan to leave in May. It really was beyond a plan now; it was an obsession; there was no doubt in my mind that it was going to happen. In January, I also began my new job at H&R Block, working in the evenings and weekends, which left little time for much else except reading and writing music. For Christmas, I received another book by James Michener, *Iberia*, which was a history of Spain. After reading the Drifters I became very interested in spending time in that country.

Also, as the new year began, I moved out of the little house on Cypress Street and found a nice room with a kitchenette at the Coast Motel on Newport Boulevard. It was an old one-story structure, probably built in the early 50's with maybe 14 units that were positioned away from the busy boulevard beyond a large greenbelt. It was cozy and certainly good enough for what I needed for the next four months.

I was not totally sure about Christina. We had spent Sunday after New Year's Day together at her parent's house and I knew I liked her but was not sure if the relationship would really launch. It had been over two years since I had a real relationship, not counting Carole. Christina was in Fresno; I was in Newport and I was determined not to let anything get in the way of my plans to go to Europe.

The weekend after New Year's, I drove to San Diego to see my friend Ed Davis, who was attending the University of San Diego. I learned later that while I was gone, Christina and a friend of hers drove down to Newport and was looking for me at Anaheim Street, which was still my mailing address. Tom, who was now back from his road trip across the US, relayed the information to me and I realized that she was very interested in pursuing us being together. I still had not started work at H&R Block by the second week of January, so I called her and made a date to go out the following weekend in Fresno.

We ended up going to the movies to see a double feature; both of which took place in Europe. One of the movies called "Friends", portrayed a young man meeting a girl, falling in love and running away together from Paris to an empty farmhouse in rural France. With music by Elton John and gorgeous cinematography I was moved by the romance of the couple as well as inspired by the beauty of the French countryside. I realized I wanted to have both.

The following week I began working at Block so I would now be limited to Fresno trips on weekends. That did not deter Christina, who I now called Chris and who came down to stay with me at the Coast Motel. Like the movie, our friendship grew, and we became lovers. I wrestled with the dilemma of leaving in May for six months, wondering if our relationship could survive that kind of absence. Finally, one day while she was visiting for the weekend, I said to her, "Would you like to go to Europe with me?"

I believe she was pleasantly surprised and responded that she was taking classes and would not have the money to pay her way. It was love that inspired me to ask her to go but I made it clear I would not have the money to support both of us on the trip. My resolve for the trip was beyond love. As the weeks slipped by, she began to find solutions that could possibly allow her to meet me mid-summer. She would continue to work part-time, attend summer school, which lasted until the middle of July, and be able to save enough money for a flight and three months of living expenses. It appeared as if I would travel alone from May to the end of July, then have a companion for the three months that followed.

In March, I stopped in at a Travel Agency that was situated next to my bank on 17th Street in Cost Mesa. Over the past few months I had looked at the window dressing with exotic pictures of all the many destinations of the world and decided this is where I would purchase my ticket to Amsterdam, the same destination that had been my introduction to Europe in 1969. May was only six weeks away and I was told it would be less expensive to buy well in advance of my departure. The woman behind the counter was very helpful and together we chose KLM as the carrier leaving in the evening of May 1st and arriving non-stop to Amsterdam the following late afternoon. I had a return ticket without a departure date as I had no idea when I would return. Six months was the plan as long as my money lasted.

On March Twelfth, The United Rubber Workers chose to strike at Voit. There had been tension for some time; as I recall it had to do with holidays or vacation time, which was all insignificant to me since this job was only a means to an end and I was very close to the end. The strike, though, did mean having time off but also no money. If it continued for any length of time, I would be a bit short of my goal since I only had four more paydays before I left. I thanked the wisdom for deciding to work at Block which gave me extra money in case the strike was not settled. Fortunately, it was worked out in just two weeks.

By April, I decided it was time to buy my travel gear. I chose Grant's Camping and Ammo Shop on Newport Boulevard just a couple miles from the Coast Motel and chose a light Down Sleeping Bag and a lightweight backpack. I also picked up what was called a tube tent, which was nothing more than thick plastic sheeting that could serve as ground cover or if strung between two trees could work as a tent As it turned out it was a great asset on the trip. I found a pair of square toed boots with brass buckles that I really like. Since bell bottom pants were in style the boots were perfect. I also bought a new pair of moccasins which was my casual wear for the past year. I planned taking a couple of T-shirts, blue of course, a long-sleeved work shirt, (popular at the time but nothing more than a farm labor shirt), and two pairs of pants; Levi's and a bit dressier cotton denim. I had one pair of shorts and one bathing suit, a sweater, and a suede jacket that I found and purchased somewhere and absolutely loved. Adding a couple of pairs of socks and five pairs of underwear, I was complete.

My objective was to travel as light as possible, with the idea of being able to wash clothes at campgrounds or hostels. The process of deciding what to take only increased my excitement which expanded as each day passed. The plans that I had made the past year were about to unfold. I don't think there is any better feeling than the realization of a dream and this one was mine.

At the end of March as the strike ended, I gave my two weeks' notice at Voit. It had been nearly a year and I was grateful for both the experience and the money. My life had changed in many ways from my first day on the job, all for the better. April 12th was my last day. I said goodbye to the friends I had made, realizing they were work friends and I would probably never see them again. Most of the guys wished me well, were a bit envious but gracious. A couple thought I was crazy to waste my money on such a frivolous pursuit, but I just attributed that to jealousy. As I walked out of the plant for the final time, I felt an exhilaration knowing I had accomplished something very special.

In 1972, April 15th was on a Saturday, which made our last day at H&R Block a Monday the 17th. It was late evening when I closed my little office in the shopping center where I had worked since January, a retail site on Harbor Boulevard. I had worked with an older woman, Molly Jackson, who gave me two shiny new silver dollars as a going away gift. One of them I still have; the other I would give away as a gift to a Flamenco Dancer in Portugal.

As I left the office, I breathed in the cool spring air and thought I would burst with excitement and a wonderful feeling of freedom. I had my ticket, my money, and two weeks to say goodbye to friends from San Diego to Fresno. I planned on going to the main office of Block to attend the "end of tax season" party but before I did, I walked to a pay-phone in the shopping center and called Chris. "I did it," I said. She congratulated me. My senses were soaring; I had overcome devastation with Carole and money, only to be at this point with nothing ahead but adventure, travel and a young woman who loved me and was congratulating me. I told her, I would see her on Thursday; that I was going to San Diego for a few days to say goodbye to friends and we said goodbye to each other. It was time to celebrate for so many reasons.

The next morning, I loaded my car with all my possessions from the room at the Coast Motel. There was no need to pay anymore rent; I was done with Newport and Costa Mesa. Tom and I had lunch at Coco's as a goodbye and then I drove to San Diego to see Ed Davis and old Fresno friends who now lived there, Ken and Linda Wilson. The sense of freedom that I felt as I drove south on the 405 was the best of all feelings or emotions. I was in the moment; nowhere I had to be and nothing I had to do.

I was in San Diego only two nights then headed north to Fresno. Those last few days were filled with dinners with my parents and Christine's family followed by a surprise going away party; given by my folks who invited all my Fresno friends and family.

On the last day of April, a Sunday, Chris and I spent the day together; walking, talking and discussing her plans to join me in late July in Amsterdam. I had set an itinerary that would allow her to send letters to various cities at the American Express Offices and we promised to write. How strange it was to me, that I finally had a girlfriend after so long and now I was about to leave her for nearly three months.

In 1972, May 1st was on a Monday. My flight from Los Angeles to Schiphol Airport in Amsterdam was scheduled to leave at 8 pm and my parents planned to take me along with Chris to the airport. My dad took off from his Insurance Office early so we could arrive in LA in time to have dinner with my Grandmother, and Aunt and Uncle who all lived in L.A. and wanted to see me off. There were no security checks in those days so families could walk you all the way to the departure gate to say their final goodbyes.

My parents could never understand my attraction to Europe, but they were there to support me and that meant a lot to me. It was a time in my life of family and close friendships; a time of possibilities of a future unknown, of people not yet known to me and adventures to be lived. At the departure gate I thanked the family for coming to say goodbye, kissed Christina and walked through the gate to the corridor leading to the plane that would carry me to my beloved Europe and experiences that would forever change the way I saw the world.

Chapter 23

AMSTERDAM IN 1972, for a young man, was the essence of vibrant, multi-cultural and multi-generational energy. The country of Holland is surrounded by Germany on the east, Belgium on the southern border and exposed to the North Sea on the north and western edges. When I was there in 1969, I fell in love with the people; some of the warmest human beings I had ever met. I was fascinated at the wonderful streets with buildings of unique architecture, old but not outdated and checkered with the picturesque canals. Of course, of all the memories of this wonderful city, Marta was the one that left me not wanting to leave three years before and beckoning me to return as I finally did. But time has a way of changing circumstances and memories. I had no idea how to find her again, nor would I recognize her if I saw her. It was one night that seemed more like a dream than reality; still against hope, I resolved to look.

My plane touched down at Schiphol Airport late in the afternoon and my first objective, after going through immigration, was to find a place to stay for the first night. My intention was to go to the bed and breakfast that Jerry and I had stayed in 1969. I still had their address but did not have a map or memory of how to find it, so I overspent on a taxi from the airport. I certainly couldn't continue to splurge like that if I was to stay in Europe for six months. My budget was ten dollars a day and that would take some creativity to accomplish and this taxi ride was a full day's budget.

We arrived at the address I had given the driver, and as he drove away, I thought of the scene on this exact spot three years before when Marta drove away. I turned and rang the bell. The latch buzzed indicating I could open the door. I climbed the stairs arriving to an awkward reunion as the mother and daughter, Lotte and Sophie, smiled at me without recognition. It took a few minutes, but finally, because I was a young American from California it came back to them. I was invited to sit down and offered coffee and cookies.

Did they have a room available, I asked? No, they were completely full, but they would recommend a reasonable hotel and call for me for a reservation.

We settled into a nice conversation of lives over the last three years. Theirs was pretty much the same; probably as it had been since they began the bed and breakfast so many years ago after the mother's husband had passed away. I told them about my adventures over that same period, leaving out my aborted marriage to Carole which embarrassed me and was still a source of pain. American politics was always interesting to most Europeans and President Nixon as well as the continuing war in Viet Nam was always substance for lively discussions. The afternoon was becoming evening when I told them I would be going and promised to call when I returned in July. They gave me directions to the bus stop and which bus to take to the Beethoven Hotel where I had my one and only reservation for the entire time of this European adventure.

The only thing I remember about this hotel was that the guests appeared to be mostly businessmen rather than tourists and that my room was incredibly small. I set out immediately after checking in to find something to eat. The old standby, Wimpy's was within a couple of blocks and being tired and a bit jet lagged, I decided to eat there to celebrate my reunion back to this marvelous city. After eating I walked for about an hour and exhausted, I went back to the hotel very tired but very happy.

My plan was to stay about five days in Amsterdam and rediscover the memories of various places I had visited. As I sat in a hotel's basement cafeteria, eating my complimentary breakfast that first morning, I observed the many businessmen of all ages in their suits and ties as they ate, discussing presumably business in a language I did not understand. It occurred to me that at 24, I could very well be part of that group in America but instead, fate had allowed me to be free of that, at least for that present time. Although I did not have any feeling of superiority about that freedom, I certainly was grateful.

My first task that morning was to be the same in each city I visited; get a city map, which could usually be found in bookstores, train stations or travel agencies. Once I got my bearings, I would walk for miles, discovering points of interest and various neighborhoods. It took me nearly two days to re-familiarize myself with Amsterdam as well as the bus and tram system. I found the Central Train Station, the Rijksmuseum and the famous red-light district, De Wallen. I also needed to find a hostel that would be more affordable than the hotel I was staying in; I hated to give up the comfort but staying on my budget was going to be the key for a longer stay. I thought of Sean, whom Jerry and I traveled with in 1969; how did he survive for as long as he did on practically no money? I did not want to be that austere, but I was going to be as frugal as possible. My meals would often be sandwiches of French bread, ham, cheese, and tomato which I could eat at a park. By the second day, I discovered an automat where I could purchase ramen noodles and pork, which was cheap but very satisfying.

In the two days I roamed around this amazing city, I never met a soul. I went to the red-light district at night, only to find Marta. Even though I didn't believe I would find her, it was interesting to see again this incredible display as I walked along the avenue looking at beautiful women as if they were mannequins in a department store window. I could not recall the exact location that Marta and I had met and after a while I realized it was a futile effort. I hoped that she was alright, wherever she was and whatever she was doing; a soul that came into my life for a moment in time to make an impression that would last a lifetime. There would be many in my life; there already had been. As I walked back to the hostel that second night, I realized, you cannot re-create the past; you can only keep moving forward.

After two days, I had seen all that I wanted to see. I felt a bit of disappointment; the glamor that I remembered was not to be found on this visit; probably because I was alone. Most people in Holland speak English so the language was not as much of an issue as my own shyness. On the third day, I took a train to the outskirts of the city to Van Lith, a small town that featured the famous windmills and views of some of the dykes. The best part of that trip was just watching out the window of the train as it moved away from the city and into the countryside. Since it was early May, I got to see the fields of Tulips, a virtual color parade of yellow, orange, red and purple. I wondered what they did with all those flowers; there were thousands of them.

On Friday, my fourth day I went back to the train station and bought a ticket to Zandvoort, a beach community along western Holland on the North Sea. It was too cold still to swim or sunbathe, so I just walked along the shore and spent the day reading a mystery novel I had purchased. I would discover, throughout my early days of travel, that even though I would become lonely, there was a peace and comfort at the shore of an ocean or sea. The next day was Saturday and it was time to move south to Paris.

The wonderful part of traveling without a tight itinerary is when something happens to change plans; it is easy to make the change. And, so it was as I tried to leave Amsterdam. I woke early Saturday morning, excited at the anticipation of hitchhiking all the way to Paris. I still had my original Michelin Map of Europe and located with the help of my city map where I needed to go, to catch the main highway that would lead me south through Holland and Belgium to Paris. I rode the city bus to the outskirts of the city and estimated where I should start hitchhiking. Still in a residential area, I boldly put my thumb out to see if I could get a ride. It only took a few minutes before someone stopped. He was going only a short distance, about 10 km further out of the city. Where was I going, he asked? I told him Paris.

"You are American. I can tell by the way you are dressed." Because it was a brisk morning, I had on my jeans, sweater and my suede jacket. He asked questions about America and California until he announced, "this is where I exit."

The highway we were on was in the suburbs and the turnoff on the flat terrain was only twenty feet from the highway. I thanked the driver, got out and had, really, no idea where I was; wondering if I could even get a ride from such a remote location. The first one had been easy. Standing there, with my pack on the ground, a feeling of insecurity hit me followed by the realization that I had to pee. There was a bush nearby and I walked away from my pack to relieve myself behind the bush.

Finishing, I walked back to where my pack was and noticed a car pulling to a stop in front of where it lay. I hadn't even had a chance to put out my thumb. My thought was; this is someone to tell me I can't hitchhike here but as I approached the car a younger, nice looking man leaned toward the open passenger window from the driver's side and said, "You speak English", which was more of a statement that a question.

"Yes"

"Do you want a ride?"

"Yes, I'm going to Paris."

"Ok, I'm not going that far but I can take you about sixty kilometers."

The car was a current model Peugeot 4 door sedan. I opened the back door and lay my backpack on the back seat, then got in the front and he sped away. I thought to myself that this hitchhiking was not as difficult as I thought. But then, this was Holland a very friendly country. His name was Aad, pronounced Ed. As we talked, I learned he was a high school geography teacher and lived in the suburban area of Amsterdam called Delft. He was on his way to spend the afternoon with his parents who lived in the countryside. Aad was in his early 30's and reminded me of Joe Truner, the high school teacher who first introduced me to the idea of going to Europe. We talked about his job and he gave me interesting facts about the Netherlands and Amsterdam. I told him that I had just arrived a few days before and was planning on staying for six months.

The drive was pleasant; he was interesting and easy to talk to. As we approached the turnoff to his parent's home, he asked if I would like to stay and have lunch with his family before carrying on to Paris. "Why not", I thought. I had no timetable; it would be good to be with people again and a free meal was not bad either.

"That would be wonderful", I said, "if it's ok with your parents".

"Absolutely" he said, "they are very gracious people and besides, getting to talk to an American will be a special treat for them."

I don't remember much about the day; I met his mother and father and a younger brother, and I was treated like a guest of honor. It was a nice Saturday afternoon where we spent most of the time in their backyard, which was not fenced, but rather open to a forest of trees beyond the grass lot. How the Europeans loved to talk about American Politics, which was always fun for me to exchange my thoughts, liberal as I was at that time, it resonated well with European attitudes. As the afternoon became late, I began to wonder how difficult it would be to get a ride from this little village and that it was still a few hours before I would reach Paris. I kept those thoughts to myself because I was enjoying the day and my visit, and I really liked Aad. I pushed the worrisome thoughts from my mind and resolved to just be in the moment. This was Europe and I had been fortunate enough to experience being with a family.

As Aad's mother and father cleared the table and moved inside he said to me, "Why don't you stay with me for a few days in Amsterdam? I will have to begin work on Monday, but you would have a place to stay and I can show you some of the areas around the city".

I thought about it for a moment; this was not my plan but then since I had no rigid plans and no one waiting for me, I was completely free to alter my course and what a great opportunity. I could also save money by not paying rent. I liked Aad, he was older, and he was cool. I said, "Sure if you don't mind having me."

"No of course not, otherwise I wouldn't ask. By the way, though, I must tell you that I am gay."

So, there it was, I thought. In a flash it all came together. His parents must have figured I was a new toy he had picked up. That was why he picked me up. I responded, "By the way, I'm not so if that is your idea then I better not stay with you."

"No, no", he said emphatically; "I figured you were not gay, and I promise I won't have any expectations."

My mind continued thinking, just my luck; a perfect opportunity but all the sudden not so perfect. Still, he appeared to be a kind person and I knew I could handle myself if it got weird.

"Ok", I said, "thank you".

We drove back to Amsterdam and our conversation centered around his homosexuality. I had not known an openly gay person and always wondered how and why someone would choose that path. He told me as far back as he could remember he knew he was different. He did not care to play with soldiers as a child but liked dolls. He said that it was something he was born with as most gay or lesbian individuals were. It wasn't anything he would have chosen because it was very difficult to be different. When he came out with the truth, his parents were heat broken. Eventually they accepted it, but he knew in many ways it just was not the same; he was radically different than they were, and he was constantly aware that he had hurt them. But he was who he was and in a city like Amsterdam, which was very liberal and open minded, he was accepted. I had always had a stereotype visual of gay men being somewhat feminine in their demeanor, yet Aad did not fit that image at all. He was quite masculine, like a Paul Newman character and while the fact that he was gay was part of my awareness, I did not dwell on it.

Staying with Aad turned out to be positive overall but also a bit uncomfortable, not because he was gay but because I was in his world and was a little unsure of myself. On Sunday, we went for a drive through the fields of Tulips that were being harvested. All those colorful flowers were now in piles of still brilliant colors like stacks of hay in the field. I learned from Aad that the flowers were not the crop, but the bulbs were the true cash crop of these farms. We saw the dykes and Aad explained the history and geography of the Netherlands. Holland, I learned was really a province; one of twelve in the Netherlands, which means "low country". Much of the country is below sea level and thus the systems were created that included, dykes, canals and pumping stations. The windmills that are sprinkled throughout the countryside and what has become a symbol of Holland, are used to pump water out of areas below sea level. Amsterdam is the Capital of the Netherlands, but Den Hague is the government seat.

We drove for some time and because the information Aad was giving me that day was the subject he knew about, it was almost too much to absorb. It was a good thing there would not be a test the following day. By mid-day we ended up along the coastal town of Bergan Aan Zee, which translates to Bergen Beach. It was a very quant seaside resort that I never would have discovered on my own. We had lunch at a little restaurant with outside dining and partial views of the sea. As we ate, we continued to talk about life and philosophy; a subject that I always enjoyed, and Aad did as well.

Later that evening we sat in Aad's living room watching a talk show on the BBC (British Broadcasting Service), and Aad told me about a recent talk show he had seen. There was a famous actress on the show discussing her philosophy of life and what she said was that *"unpleasant feelings are never necessary and never to be justified."* For me, statements like that strike a chord in my soul. I was so taken by those words that I asked him to write them down for me, which he did and I still have them in a pocket calendar that I carried with me that year. The statement became my mantra as I traveled and evolved to be permanently part of my life's philosophy.

Aad's apartment located in the suburbs outside of Amsterdam was a tidy two-bedroom flat that allowed me to have my own room, although we did share a bathroom. The transportation system made it easy for me to go into the city during the hours that he was at school. Every night, it seemed, he had plans for us; he was a perfect host. One evening, we drove to another small berg outside of Amsterdam to have dinner with some very good friends of his, Peter and his wife Sarah. Throughout dinner and after dinner drinks we discussed world affairs. As always, the people I met loved Americans but did not like our President, Richard Nixon. Peter, a short, stout young man who wore a full, heavy red beard was very strong in his opinions and tended to raise his voice with the passion of his convictions. At times he would slip into Dutch and it would remind me that English was not any of their first language. Fortunately, their English was so fluent; I would forget I was in a foreign country.

The last night at Aad's was a Wednesday and he had a night class until 9 p.m., so before class, he dropped me off in front of a night club he wanted to show me when he finished teaching that evening. I had nearly 3 hours to wait so I took advantage of the time to enjoy a pleasant spring evening walking the canal laced neighborhoods, reminding myself once again what a lovely place Amsterdam was and how fortunate I was to spend more time here. I had been here since I arrived, nine days, much longer than I had planned. Meeting Aad had certainly been a bonus because I had experienced much more of this wonderful place than I otherwise would have. I planned on coming back to meet Christina in July, but Aad would be on holiday the week I planned to return. I figured at this point he was tired of entertaining me and since I was not Gay there was no benefit for him, but he was always a gentleman and I liked him very much.

By 9 o'clock I returned to our meeting place in the square that was surrounded by little shops at each side of the night club. Trees in the square were decorated with twinkling lights creating a lovely Van Gough like setting. As I sat on a bench admiring the scene, a pair of hands from behind, covered my eyes; it was Aad expressing the playful side of this button-down teacher.

"Come", he said, "let's go in so you can see what it's like in a Gay and Lesbian nightclub". And so, this 24 year old boy witnessed a slice of life I had never experienced before; men dancing with each other, some kissing and some in drag so well done it was difficult to tell if they were men or women. There were women in the club as well; some quite beautiful but they were certainly not looking at me. The men, however, were looking at me, and suddenly I realized what a woman must feel like in a room full of single men and it made me uncomfortable. We found a table and as Aad talked to people he knew, I just sat and watched this amazing demonstration of humanity; not in judgement, but rather in wonder, while hoping I would not get hit on. But Aad never left me alone and, of course, I more than likely gave off the vibe that I was straight. At one point while we were there, I realized I had to go to the bathroom and also became aware that I might be safer going to the women's rather than the men's. I asked Aad what to do and he laughed. "You go to the men's; I will go with you, so you don't have to worry." He did and I was fine.

We stayed at the club for only an hour. Aad would have to work in the morning and he wanted to take me to the train station in the morning before he went to his classes. I was finally going to Paris and because I had saved money living with Ed the past five nights, I could afford to take the train.

The next morning, I woke earlier than normal so I could shower and be ready when Aad took me to the Central Train Station. I did not know it at the time what a luxury it was to have a shower every morning and a comfortable bed each night. I had yet to camp out; that adventure lay ahead. The difficult part of traveling is saying goodbye to people you meet who become friends; especially when the goodbye is most likely forever. I never have forgotten Aad's kindness and friendship. In 1972 there was not anything we heard of called HIV/AIDS. I wondered when that became a world epidemic for mostly gay men what happened to Aad. I wrote to him once but never received a reply. I have often hoped he has had or did a good life.

Chapter 24

THE TRAIN TO Paris was somewhat full. I walked along the outer aisle looking into the individual box like spaces on my left that served up to six people; three on each side facing each other, looking for empty seats. European trains are so comfortable and efficient, and I looked forward to the ride. The cars on this train were quite different than the ones that I took to the beach areas, which were more like bus seats set in rows. I found a section that was nearly empty, so I lifted my backpack up over my head to the shelf above the seat and then sat down by the window. Eventually other people filled the empty seats so that by the time the train lurched forward there were only two empties in our cabin. The other seats were occupied by two young men who appeared to be American and an older, well dressed gentleman. The Americans were quite well-absorbed in themselves, chattering away about just barely making it to the train on time and the adventure they were apparently on for the next couple of weeks. I would eventually learn they had both recently graduated from college and were on this trip as a reward before returning to their post-college life. They seemed a bit immature, or maybe I was being too critical, but for whatever reason I chose not to engage with them. I settled in my space and looked out the window as the city of Amsterdam melted away and the beautiful green fields of the country re-appeared once again.

My thoughts of my adventure so far and my time with Aad made me smile to myself; realizing this was only the beginning. Aad had been a gentleman in every way and I considered myself lucky to have had the experience to get to know him. I had little knowledge about Gay individuals and now understood the prejudice that people had toward them. Their life was not just a choice, but rather physical from birth. Here was a man who was kind, classy and intelligent who happened to be Gay. I decided that his sexual orientation was not a sin as some religions believed, but rather, just how he was born. I considered myself lucky that I had not had to carry that burden of society's judgement; it surely must have been a struggle.

I turned my attention to the two Americans. They continued to be a bit too loud and obnoxious; like a couple of 10-year old's on a field trip. The older French gentleman sitting next to me I sensed, was tiring of these two characters. Finally, after about thirty minutes he stood up, snatched his valise from the overhead compartment and quietly left to find a better group of seatmates leaving the three of us alone. That is when the tall American with curly almost black hair began to ask me questions in the usual "getting to know you" manner. Where was I from? Why was I here? How long had I been traveling? The answers I gave him sufficiently impressed these guys who were here for only a couple of weeks from New York and were amazed I was traveling alone and planning to stay six months. I had not thought too much about the fact that what I was doing was a bit out of the ordinary but then, I had discovered in my adult life, that I was different. When I attended college for a business degree, my classmates were locked into getting career jobs right out of college. For most of them, a trip like this was not an option, which was also true for these guys. The tall American introduced himself as Audie and his sidekick, Steve. They were similar to my college mates who would not step off the path; this trip was their opportunity to wander off momentarily and they were going to have fun; which was fine but for me they were just too goofy. So, when Audie, the leader of the two, suggested I join them when we arrived in Paris, I began to think of excuses for escaping.

Paris is a city like no other and my first look as we walked out of the train station upon our arrival that afternoon was one of wonder. What caught my attention were the old gray buildings with balconies incased in iron fences, so different than the city of Amsterdam. I had no map, nor did I have any knowledge of this massive city or where I was going to stay. The two Americans followed me and together we set out to find a cheap hotel. Because at the time I did not know where we were, I have no memory where we walked but based on the location of the train station I can estimate approximately the neighborhoods we walked in; me with my back pack and them with their suitcases. We arrived at the Gare du Nord Station in the north-east section of the city, and it was as if I had been swallowed up in this amazingly enormous city. We walked for a couple of miles and then somehow, fortuitously, the young Americans decided to go their separate way. It was probably because they realized I was not going to stay in the kind of hotel they wanted and my taste at that moment was only austere.

As I would discover repeatedly, being alone can be lonely but it has a special freedom that is lost when being with others. I continued walking south on major streets paying as much attention to the beautiful women of Paris as I was to any possible tourist attraction. The weather that day in May was wet and cold but I was able to keep warm with layers of clothes from T-shirt, to sweater, to my Suede Jacket and even though I did not know where I was, I was caught in the moment, enjoying the sights and sounds of this incredibly vibrant city.

As it turned out I found an old hotel somewhere on the north side of the Seine River called the Maxim Hotel. It was not the kind of place that well healed tourists would check in to, but for this young vagabond it was perfect. Everything about the Maxim indicated life in another time, perhaps during the early 1900's with only the electrical systems changed but not much else. My room, of course was small, with ceilings as high as the room was long, but it was all I needed. I discovered that when checking into a hotel, I had to hand over my passport for them to keep until I checked out. This at first made me nervous but eventually I realized that it was what they did and that it was perfectly safe. Once I got to my room, I dropped my backpack on the floor and set out for an early evening discovery of Paris.

I began walking south to a bridge that crossed the River Seine. As I crossed and stopped midway, I looked to my right and could see the Eifel Tower in the distance. In the next three days, I would spend hours walking the city finding the Notre-Dame and the Louvre on the West Bank. I would discover the Champs-Elyles and the Arc de Triumph on the north's higher rent district as well as the shops, the Opera House and the American Express Office to get my first letter from Christina. I noticed also, many younger men and women outside the American Express selling used cars. One young man, holding a cardboard sign with "for sale" in English was trying to sell an older Renault and I stopped to ask what this was all about. He explained that travelers, like himself bought these used cars, drove all over the European Continent and then sold the car for nearly what they paid for it. It was an inexpensive way to travel. The idea was intriguing, and I made a mental note to consider it before Christina arrived in Europe in July.

For me, being in a place like Paris was for the experience and discovery and not the education going into the museums and the Eiffel Tower. One of the reasons was I did not want to spend the money for admission but even more than that; I loved just absorbing the city and the people who were part of the multi-cultural persona that was Paris. Aside from the short conversation with the English-speaking young man who was trying to sell his car, I talked to nobody. I spent each day walking; resting at times in one of the many parks that were scattered throughout the city; observing older men, who reminded me of Maurice Chevalier in the movie *Gigi*. As always, I got a map and continued to walk, got lost and then found my way back with the Seine serving as a landmark to navigate from. On the third day, a Sunday, I took the metro to the Boise de Boulogne, a massive park at the southern end of the city that is nearly three times the size of New York's Central Park. Observing families spending quiet time picnicking or just strolling through the lush gardens, I wished at that moment, I had someone with me to share this experience.

Travel is a great microcosm for life. There are days that work and are fun and days that are challenging but always it is about the experience. Paris was more of an experience, not necessarily all positive but, interesting. I concluded it was time to move on although I was not sure where to go next; I just knew I wanted to head south and get to Spain. Before leaving Paris, I wanted to see the King's Chateau in Versailles. I gathered my possessions checked out of my hotel and set out to hitchhike to Versailles. I soon realized that this was a whole different experience than hitchhiking in Holland. It was Monday and while it took nearly an hour, I finally got a ride from a businessman heading further south; he dropped me off at the edge of this little town, Versailles, and drove on. I made my way to where the palatial Chateau was located, but because I traveled more by impulse than preparation, I failed to know that Monday was the one day of the week the palace was closed. I peered through the iron fence to get a look at what I had missed. Many years later, I would have the opportunity to visit this opulent palace with lavish furnishings and gardens built under the Monarchy of Louis XIV, moving the aristocracy from the squalor of Paris. The separation from the city and from classes became the eventual death of the Monarchy in France when during Louis XVI and his family, were overthrown, during the French Revolution. Apparently living with that kind of luxury while people were starving was not a smart way to rule.

It was late afternoon and I decided to save money by not getting a room for the night. I walked a few blocks until I found a bakery and bought a loaf of that wonderful fresh, French bread. I then found a delicatessen and purchased slices of cheese and Salami. This would be my dinner and as I walked back to a park near the palace, I decided if there were no police to stop me, I would spend the night there. I had been in Europe now for two weeks and had not slept in the sleeping bag I had attached to my backpack. I hoped it would be warm enough because as the day surrendered to evening the temperature dropped and soon also, the rain began to fall. Here I was, alone in a foreign country, somewhat homeless at the moment, wondering if I would be able to stay the night, without being told to move on or worse, arrested. I strung a clothesline, I was carrying in my pack, through the plastic tube tent and secured it between two trees, allowing enough slack to create a tent with an opening on both ends. It wasn't the best on a wet night like this but once I crawled into my sleeping bag, I was warm enough and managed to stay dry throughout the night.

The next morning, I was determined to continue to hitchhike. Patience was not one of my strong qualities then, nor is it still. I don't like to wait, and hitchhiking is a waiting game, especially in France. I don't remember how long it took to get the first ride out of Versailles, or how many rides it took to get to my destination, Tours, which was about 200 Kilometers from Versailles. I do know, though, it took me all day to go as far as it would take a train a little over an hour to reach the same destination. I was tired, lonely and a bit discouraged.

I had not slept that well the night before and made up my mind I would stay in a hotel in Tours. I managed to get a good night's rest and woke the following day refreshed and ready to get back on the road thinking surely, I would fare better than I had the day before. I was wrong, it was worse, but the day would prove to be eventful.

I was not eating very much since arriving in France. Restaurants were expensive so mostly I survived on the bread, ham, salami and cheese. I was losing weight; I could tell by my pants that seemed to be getting bigger. My budget, each day, was made up with choices; food, transportation and where to sleep. I couldn't have it all, so I had to choose. My morning in Tours, like most hotels in Europe, provided a nice breakfast buffet. I knew if I ate as much as I could, I could be ok for several hours.

With a fresh resolve that I would get a ride this day I walked to the main road where I had been dropped off the day before. My destination was Bordeaux, which was nearly 350 Kilometers, almost twice the distance I had traveled the day before. It was early enough to catch commuters heading to work, maybe I would get lucky. With my pack and rolled up sleeping bag sitting at my feet, I put on a friendly and alert face and held out my right thumb. Still cars were flashing by and no one stopped. What was wrong with these French people? Finally, after about 20 minutes, someone pulled over. I picked up my bag and ran to the waiting car. The window was open, and he said something in French. I yelled back "No parlez-vous Francis". I'm sure I didn't look French with my American clothes but who knows why anyone would stop for a long-haired young man, especially a business man.

"Where are you going?" he said in heavily accented English.

"Bordeaux."

"Get-in, I can take you as far as Poitiers, one hundred Kilometers."

So, I rode with him, mostly in silence on the main highway to Poitiers where he left me on the side of the highway. I thanked him as I stepped out of the car. Well that wasn't so bad, I thought. It was mid-morning and I walked along the road that was more like a country-side avenue than a highway, with a grassy embankment lined with Cypress Trees and far less traffic than what I had seen earlier in Tours. Further down the road, I could see two figures that also appeared to be hitchhiking. From the distance I could not tell if it was a man and a woman or two men; one was tall and the other much shorter. I had not counted on competition but at least I was first.

The sun was out, and it was a pleasant warm day with fortunately, no rain. As the day slowly passed, I watched cars stream by with none stopping. I am sure if I was not such an impatient guy and had learned to be in the moment at that time in my life, I could have just enjoyed the experience, but I was not enjoying it at all. I looked down at my competition and they were not having any luck either. After a couple of hours, I was getting bored and a little hungry. I kept turning to see if the couple, down the road was still there; finally noticing they were walking toward me. As they neared, I noticed the short one was a college aged man, probably younger than me but not much. His friend, who was almost as tall as me, was kind of goofy looking, not handsome like his friend but unique, with large facial features. The two of them could have been right out of central casting in some comedy or cartoon. The short one spoke first, but I had no idea what he said.

"Do you speak English?" I said.

"A little," he replied, "not much." His friend the tall goofy one just stared.

Through the kind of communication that occurs when you cannot understand each other's language, I finally figured out that they were going to visit some friends at the University of Bordeaux. At first, they assumed I was from England but when they realized I was American, they became impressed. They were not used to seeing Americans like me in the middle of France, hitchhiking. They were going to go into the town and get something to eat. The short one's name was Alain who did all the talking, said they were tired of waiting for a ride. They lived in Poitiers and had been on the side of the road since early morning. They decided now, to take a train; would I like to join them? At this point I was so tired of waiting that I jumped at the opportunity and since I had no idea where the train station was, I considered the offer a fortunate coincidence.

We walked into the small town to a café where we had lunch, then walked a few more blocks to the train station. I don't recall when it was decided that I would go with them to the University but that was what happened. The ticket to Bordeaux was twenty-five francs, about five dollars, which was half my day's budget. While I was conscious of spending the money, I also made the decision that if I had to cut short this trip because I ran out of money, I was ok. I did not want to spend my whole summer waiting for free rides, especially in France.

The next 24 hours became an adventure within my journey that was to become one of the more memorable of my experiences that year in Europe. It was odd, traveling with two new companions, when communication was limited to only the most basic words. I was able to figure out that they had friends at the University and that John Mayell Blues Breakers were playing that night; the main reason they were going. Alain continued to try to communicate until the novelty wore off, and then along with his buddy, who never tried to communicate with me, just stared out the window at the passing countryside.

We arrived at the Bordeaux Station late in the afternoon and shared a cab to the University. The first thing I noticed as we arrived at the campus was a sign on one of the dormitory's that had the name Nixon with x in his name a swastika. Nixon was not a popular president in Europe. We were met by an attendant at the entrance to the dormitory, who was able to tell us which room Alain's friends were staying. We climbed two flights of stairs to a third floor, found the room and Alain knocked. The door was opened, and I awkwardly followed my companions into the room as two students greeted Alain and his buddy in excited dialog, none of which I understood. Alain then introduced me to the students, one who spoke English well enough for us to be able to communicate. They seemed amazed that they had an American in their dorm and for the moment I felt like some kind of celebrity. While it was cool that they were so impressed with having me there I began to wonder, why was I here? Soon one of the students displayed a small pipe and the other three began smiling at each other.

The student who spoke English said to me, "we are going to smoke some hash, do you want to have some?"

I nodded my head thinking, why not? I was not a drug user; in fact, I had never purchased hash or pot but I had smoked it at times if someone else offered it. I decided that getting high with these guys might ease the tension I felt at the awkwardness of being there. That was another error in my thinking. I completely underestimated the strength of the hash as the pipe was passed around as well as my paranoia that arose when I got high on any kind of grass or hash. Within minutes, my brain went to another space, as at first the whole experience of being there seemed funny, like a strange movie with stranger characters. As I sat there watching I was totally amused by it all. Since the language barrier did not allow me to talk to them, watching was all I could do and, in my drug induced condition, for the moment, I was enjoying the show.

At some point the guy who spoke English asked if I would like to go with him to see some other friends in the dorm. He seemed to be the most normal of the four, including my travel companions so I agreed.

"Leave your pack here," he said.

We walked through a maze of hallways and stairs to another room and soon I found myself with entirely different people except for the one guy who had invited me to the other dorm We began drinking wine and suddenly I began to get an uncomfortable feeling again. With a rush of adrenaline, I realized, I had no idea where I was, where my backpack was and visions of this being a set-up for the three back at the first room, to rob me. My paranoia increased as I let my mind wonder if Alain had planned this from the very beginning. Then, I thought, the only thing that is really important is my money, all in traveler checks and my passport, which I always, when on the road, kept in my boot. With relief, my confidence returned. I did not want to lose my clothes and books but if I did, I would be ok. Eventually we made our way back to where Alain was, and I realized my paranoia was not a reality. These were just French students, impressed that they had an American with them, and showing me off to their friends. So, I settled into having fun at being part of the entertainment.

I became aware that the guys in the room were talking about having dinner, before the concert. There was a student cafeteria near the dormitory's that allowed the students to eat as part of their tuition. Alain and his goofy friend and I would be given passes so we could have dinner in the cafeteria. It was a great plan, but the only problem was, how could I pass for a student when I couldn't even speak French?

The student who spoke English said, "Just walk in, smile and give the guard your pass and be confident."

That sounded easy enough, so together we walked as a group to the cafeteria; all of us still quite stoned from the hash. I was struck with the craziness of being in a foreign country, unable to speak the language with people I did not know, loaded to distraction and about to walk into a cafeteria past a University Guard acting like I belonged there. The English-speaking student continued to encourage me but everyone in line knew I was American. I looked American, my clothes screamed I was American, and they all were watching me because already I was a novelty among the students, and they knew I was not going to get away with the charade. It was like some science experiment that everyone was in on and I was the experiment.

I approached the guard, full of confidence and handed him my pass with someone else's name on it. He looked at it and then at me and said something in French. I later learned he asked, "Is this your pass?"

Not knowing what he said, I did not answer, so he asked again and not wanting to be rude I said, "I don't speak French."

The boys behind me began gut laughing at the whole ridiculous con we were trying to pull off and I was sure I was about to get booted out of there, but I kept smiling, acting like I belonged there. Finally, the guard grumbled something in French, like "crazy kids", as he looked behind me at the laughing students and then looked at me and waved me through. Suddenly, I was a hero; I had done it. The boys were amazed, and I was too naïve about the situation to know it was not what they expected.

We ate dinner and then slowly made our way to some kind of gymnasium where a stage had been set up for the concert. We stayed on the floor as the lights dimmed and the concert began. The music was heavy blues with John Mayal and the Blues Breakers, the same band that Eric Clapton had played with at one time, and it was outstanding. I just stood and took in the ambience, the situation, and the music with my lingering hash high, enjoying every minute without a thought other than being in the moment. After the concert we went back to the room. The boys smoked more dope but I passed and soon fell asleep with my sleeping bag, on the floor.

The next morning, I left; I was tired of being an experiment or a novelty. Whatever it was, I was not comfortable, and it was time to get away and be alone again. There was this duality once again of preferring to be alone over being with people that I did not want to spend much time with and facing loneliness when I was alone. I said good-bye and thanked them for the hospitality and began walking toward the next adventure.

Chapter 25

IT WAS MAY 22ⁿᵈ and my third week traveling, when I finally arrived in Spain. Crossing the border from France to Spain was a mental celebration, as I believed from my reading and past experience, that it would be less expensive to travel in Spain. Now in Pamplona, I realized, I had been starving myself trying to save money and was looking forward to a good meal. A few days before, after I had left the University at Bordeaux, I checked in to a cheap hotel and spent the next two days walking in the city with a map, stopping occasionally for coffee and a snack: alone again.

At one point I found myself in a large open square; the kind that seems to be in every European City, especially in the Latin Countries. As I sat at a café watching the people, I saw a door open in a building across the square. Several men, mostly in suits, walked out and a few of them came to the café where I was sitting. One of the men approached me and asked if I was American and when I said yes, he asked if he could join me. He also was American and explained that he was attending an International Conference of geologists and engineers studying, among other things, Earthquakes. When he learned through our conversation that I was from Southern California, he raised his eyebrows and said, "From what we have heard the past couple of days, California is way overdue for a major earthquake. The San Andreas Fault is definitely going to shift to a point where California could slip into the Pacific Ocean." Over the ensuing years, of course, that has not happened. We had major earthquakes in Los Angeles and San Francisco in the 80's but nothing close to what he was describing, and over the years I have thought about what he said, but never really worried about it.

Leaving Bordeaux for Spain, my original plan was not to go to Pamplona. It was too early for the San Fermin Festival, which I planned to attend in July, but for some reason, probably because I had read so much about Pamplona, I ended up in that famous city, tired and hungry. It was late afternoon when I walked from the train station and found an inexpensive hotel, dropping off my backpack, and going out to explore what seemed more like a village.

As I walked, my focus was on food. I day-dreamed about a nice dinner while walking through the same narrow streets I would later witness the running of the bulls. As I passed each restaurant, I looked at menus and prices, deciding which one I was going to treat myself to later in the evening. I was happy to see that the prices were definitely less expensive than France. The center of the town appeared to be the Plaza del Castillo, which I would come to know simply as Castle Square. Looking at a map, the square looked like the center of a wheel, with spokes of streets extending into the town where one could find shops, restaurants and Tapas Bars. There were also bars lining one side of the square so I decided to step in to one and have a rum and Coke and try a couple of Tapas, which were small appetizers made of such delicacies as octopus, squid, sausages, egg and God only knows what else. The bar was old world, possibly the same as it was in the early 1920's, with heavy dark wood walls and a long bar with no stools. As I stood at the bar along with a crowd of Spaniards, I looked at a huge mirror that covered the wall behind the bar and noticed two things. One, all the patrons were men, and secondly, I was full head taller than all of them. At first, I was a bit self-conscious but soon got over it as I realized, no one seemed to care. I figured that it was siesta time and the men were taking a break from their work to have food and drink, before heading home for their afternoon nap.

The custom of siestas, even back then, made sense to me; stopping work for 3 to 4 hours in the middle of the day before going back to work, refreshed to continue into the late afternoon and evening. Even when I was young, I liked to take naps; afternoons seemed like a drag and naps were a great way to break up the day. I left the bar after one drink and walked along the streets looking into shop windows, which were closed during siesta hours. There was not much that really interested me until I came to a music store. Displayed in the window, on stands, were various instruments including a very pretty Spanish acoustic guitar. A vision came to me of how nice it would be, to have a guitar to play as a way of passing lonely hours. That is what I did when passing time, alone in the Coast Motel, a combination of comfort and creativity. Of course, I couldn't afford a guitar on my $10 dollar a day budget. I looked past the displayed guitar and saw that there were many guitars of lesser quality that possibly I could fit into my budget if I cut back on, what … food, travel, lodging? Or maybe just being in Spain a while, I could save money. I wanted to have a guitar in my hands again and resolved to return after siesta.

For the next couple of hours, I walked the streets of this city that Hemingway had described in his first successful novel, *The Sun Also Rises*. I walked past the bull ring and the surrounding grassy area along the Rio Arga. This was the place that the man in the picture, that first inspired me to go to Europe when I was in Newport Beach, walked in the mid-1920s. I would return in July to be part of the San Fermin Festival and the running of the Bulls. Little did I know, circumstances would have me return in July with a group of life-long friends as did Hemingway's character in his novel.

Before I returned to my hotel room for my own siesta, I passed by a restaurant that offered shrimp for a very reasonable price as well as inexpensive wine. This, I decided, was where I would have my first good meal in Spain. As I stretched out on the hotel bed, I was full of joy at the anticipation of possibly getting a guitar and having a shrimp dinner.

I slept for a while, and then read, killing time before going to dinner; figuring the restaurant would open by 6 pm. As the hour finally approached, I left the hotel and walked to the restaurant only to discover it was closed. The sign on the door, that I had missed earlier said "Abierto 20:00," (8 pm). This was an unpleasant surprise, I had not paid attention in 1969 that in Spain, people don't dine until after 8 pm. It was all part of the culture of working late after siesta, before going out for the evening. Now, with my stomach aching for food, I had to wait another two hours. I decided to head back to the music store, hoping it would be open. It was, and I walked in to look at the different guitars. I picked up one that was small, thinking about carrying it all over Europe, small would probably be better. It had nylon strings; not the metal strings I was used to, but the sound was good; good enough for what I wanted. The price was only twenty dollars; two days budget. I could make that up. The weather was warmer now so I could stay in campgrounds to catch up. This guitar would be a good companion as I traveled, so I bought it and never regretted the purchase. As it turned out I would spend many hours playing that guitar.

I took it back to my hotel room; played the many songs I knew for about an hour, until it was time to go to dinner. I imagined that at 8 pm the restaurant would be crowded, but I found myself totally alone except for the waiters. I was seated at a long table, similar to what I was used to at the Basque Restaurants I had experienced in California. There was a basket of bread on the table and I eyed it hungrily but waited until the waiter set down the menu. I already knew what I wanted, *las gambas,* (prawns). I envisioned a meal with side dishes like the Basque Restaurants, with salad and soup, beans, vegetables and French fries and possibly a dessert. I could hardly wait. I ordered the prawns and *vino tinto,* (red wine), which was served in a one-liter clay pitcher. I poured myself a glass, grabbed some bread and waited in euphoric anticipation. After about ten minutes and two more pieces of bread the waiter walked in from the kitchen with a platter of something. Must be the first course, I thought. No, it was the only course. As he sat the platter down, I realized this was my dinner; about a dozen cooked prawns, fully dressed in their shells with their eyes staring back at me. There was no rice or potatoes just shrimp. I considered ordering more food but just could not justify the expense; especially after buying the guitar.

It was close to 9 pm as I paid my bill and rose a bit unsteadily from drinking a liter of wine on an empty stomach. I was grateful for the bread which soaked up some of the wine and helped settle down my hunger. As I walked out of the restaurant, I noticed there were very few people there and I felt sorry for the owners, who had such a poor turnout. I would learn later that most people don't show up until well after 9 and closer to 10 pm. I walked for a while, disappointed by the meal but with a nice buzz from the wine and a smile on my face for the twist of fate, my naivety but knowing I had a guitar now.

I stayed in Pamplona just three days. It was still May and my plan was to explore more of Southern Spain and Portugal before returning to Pamplona for the San Fermin Festival in early July. On my second day in Pamplona I met two young guys about my age who were staying at the same hotel as me. They were traveling in Europe, taking a summer break from college in Colorado. We bought wine and sat in their room after dinner talking about life and travel and the freedom of being young with so much of life ahead. I had been playing my guitar all day – reconnecting with songs I had written while living in Costa Mesa and they had heard me and asked that I get my guitar and play a few songs. It was a nice evening and I don't remember if they were moving on the next day, but I did not see them again.

My next destination was Salamanca, only because it was one of the cities James Michener wrote about in his book Iberia. It sounded interesting and it was on my way to the Portuguese Border but, I would discover another low point in my travels as there was nothing of interest to me in Salamanca. As I got off the train, I was approached by a nice looking gentleman who asked me if I was looking for a room. I told him I was and soon we were taking his car to his home, which was a small apartment. It became a very strange situation as I was a paying guest of his family, but I was not part of the family. They were nice but our language differences made it hard to be anything other than distant. I spent hours walking the streets of Salamanca but could find nothing that really interested me and spent more time in the bedroom I was renting, playing my guitar. I think the family thought I was strange to not be out looking at tourist attractions. They probably were right. Finally, on Saturday, less than 48 hours after arriving, I was back at the train station, purchasing a ticket for Lisbon.

In the Prologue of this book, I wrote of the crossing from Spain to Portugal and of my experience with the girl in the meadow. Of course, that part of the story was fiction; a way to create the illusion of transformation to a higher consciousness that has been a goal in my life-long journey. The rest of the story though, is true and is an expression of my "hero's journey"; the search for not only meaning, but of freedom from ever-present insecurities. It was a term I took from Joseph Campbell, a 20th Century Scholar and Philosopher. I like to believe that even at 24; I had that hero's consciousness. In the first month of being in Europe, I had already experienced a great adventure; meeting Aad in Amsterdam, being in Paris and the University in Bordeaux and then Pamplona. As the month of May ended, I would spend nearly two weeks in Lisbon; the longest stay of any place I would visit. Why? Probably, because I enjoyed myself; I had a good place to stay and it was a short and inexpensive train ride to Estoril and the beach I loved to visit. I made some friendships and I found a peace and an appreciation, not only of Lisbon but of my perspective of the freedom of my own soul. It was the words Aad had told me, "unpleasant feelings are never necessary and never to be justified," that helped formulate a philosophy of life; that we have a mission to take happiness wherever we go and to whatever we do. The words I expressed to my Swiss friend, Marcus, on a warm afternoon as we stood gazing at the harbor of the Tagus River, while perched on a monument in the Palace Square; that life was meant to be enjoyed and the idea of doing anything else, "was a crime against humanity". He asked me what I meant and I explained, "When you approach people being unhappy, you spread that unhappiness; but when you are happy, you give a gift to everyone you meet". He looked at me and said, "Who are you?" and we both laughed.

Chapter 26

I DON'T RECALL how I found the Pension in Lisbon. Maybe an ad on the wall of the train station or maybe just walking into the neighborhood. I recall that this Pension was on the 2nd floor of a large building and had a dining room, and a couple of large bedrooms with several single beds. The woman, who was my host spoke very little English but had a wonderfully pleasant disposition and it was obvious she liked having young people, which was not always the case for many grumpy old Europeans. One of my roommates was a tall, lanky young man from Switzerland; maybe two years younger than me, who had been traveling about a month, as I had. His name was Marcus and he looked Swiss with tufts of blonde hair on a very angular and handsome face. Over the next four days we became very close and walked miles along the steep, hilly streets of Lisbon, that reminded me very much of San Francisco. The neighborhoods blended from residential to retail and commercial and the walks provided wonderful scenery from the changing landscape to the beautiful Portuguese people.

The weather on that last week of May was perfect. Sunny days that at times became hot, were cooled by the breezes coming off the Tagus River that served as the port of this somewhat sedate but very friendly city. It was quite different than Amsterdam or Paris and for some reason after nearly a month of travel, appealed to my senses. Marcus and I discovered a Fado music bar, the music of Portugal. The very pretty singer after performing came by our table to ask if we had anything to give her. We were just poor and dumb vagabonds so the idea of a tip to her was out of the question. I remembered though, I had two Silver Dollars in my wallet that Molly Jackson had given me in Costa Mesa and decided to give her one. She seemed to appreciate the gesture as she smiled and disappeared behind the stage.

Another wonderful discovery was the train from Lisbon to Estoril, which took less than an hour and dropped us off a short walk to a picturesque, resort beach town that I fell in love with immediately. Over the days that we spent together; our conversations often became philosophical as we tried to understand the meaning of life. As for me, having a friend to talk to as we discovered Portugal was in itself a blessing.

I became a bit concerned for Marcus after he told me that when he left Lisbon, he was going to make his way East to Turkey; his intention was to smuggle grass or hashish back across the border. I told him I had heard stories about young people attempting to do what he planned and being arrested and locked away in a Turkish Prison. He seemed cavalier about the danger and continued his stubborn insistence that he would be careful, and nothing would happen. On the first day of June he left Lisbon. We spent the morning hiking up the hill to the Castle that overlooked the city and the harbor. Then I walked with him to the train station and we had something to eat before he boarded his train. As I saw him walk away, down the platform between two trains, I prayed that he would be ok. I never saw him or heard from him again and as I have with all the friends, I made in my travels; I wished him a good life. Now I was alone again. I walked along the water's edge, looking across at a land mass in the distance. I liked it here in Lisbon and decided I would stay a few more days.

The next morning, I took another trip to Estoril for a day at the beach. Stopping on the way to the train station, I bought my usual food supply of bread, cheese and ham then at the station bought a ticket to the little beach town and while waiting for the departure time, found a detective novel in the gift shop. As always, the ocean calmed the loneliness I felt as I now faced the Atlantic Ocean. I spent the day absorbed in my book and walking along the beach. I splurged on some fries to go with my lunch and found a table to eat as I watched children playing on the beach. Alone with my thoughts it occurred to me again the contrast of loneliness and freedom. Here I was, in this wonderful country, able to do whatever I wanted and go wherever I wished. This is why for the remainder of my life; Europe would continue to represent freedom.

The train ride back to Lisbon found me staring at the countryside as the sun remained high in the late afternoon sky. I had no plans for the evening other than to take a shower at the Pension and find a place to have dinner. But as travel creates the whim of circumstances unknown to the planner, this evening was no exception. Taking the now familiar walk from the train station to the Pension, I buzzed the doorbell from the street, waiting for someone upstairs to release the latch. The hostess with her ever present smile and energy greeted me as I walked up to the upstairs flat. She then turned to continue registering two American Girls, who had apparently just arrived. The hostess paused long enough to introduce me to them. One of the girls was a bit overweight and not too friendly; her friend by contrast, had a very joyful demeanor that made me like her immediately. Her name was Lisa, her friend's name was Susan. Lisa had a pretty, fresh face and a smile that made that face light up. The three of us talked for a few minutes, gathering surface information before I asked if they had plans for dinner. The answer was no, so I asked if they would like to join me; it was Friday night and I would be happy to show them around on their first night in Lisbon. Yes, they would like that; so, we agreed to meet in the family room in an hour.

That evening, I got to know Lisa as the three of us strolled along the streets of the Pension's neighborhood where we found a small café and ordered wine with dinner. We talked for hours about life, travel and our individual histories. I learned they were from Boston and were both in college. By the end of the evening, I asked what their plans were for the next day. Susan said they had set an itinerary and planned to visit some museums. I suggested going to see the Botanical Gardens and explore the city instead. Susan said no, but to my surprise Lisa said she would like to do that. I do not think Stephanie was happy about that decision as she steadfastly clung to staying with her itinerary. As it turned out, the next day became one of those magical days that stands out as I think of my travels in Europe that year.

The years have blurred much of the details of that day, but I do remember she was very intelligent with a quick wit and sense of humor. Her wavy brown hair that hung over her shoulders and blue eyes that twinkled with joy was a combination that accentuated her beautiful demeanor. She was 20 years old, and this was her first trip to Europe. She and Susan had planned this trip for over a year and were staying only two days in Lisbon before moving on to Madrid to continue on their one-month itinerary. But for this day, we had a beautiful June Saturday to spend together that began with breakfast in the Pension kitchen of rolls, cheese and coffee. As we ate, I mapped out a walk to the Botanical Gardens. By now, I was quite familiar with the city, and decided instead of using the map we would just make our way to the Gardens and enjoy walking through the neighborhoods that were both residential and business.

We entered the front gates to the garden, and I wondered why I had chosen this, of all the sights to see because I really never was a big fan at 24 years old, of names of plants and trees. I was more interested really, just being with her. We wandered through paths, absorbing the musty smell of damp mulch, looking at an amazing display of plants, ground cover and trees; all described in Latin on little wooden signs. Soon it all looked the same to me and though she did not say so, I figured Lisa felt the same. It was much more interesting walking the streets and looking at buildings and people.

"What do you think?" I asked.

She looked at me with a serious face and said, "Very interesting," Then we both burst into laughter.

"Ok," I said, "let's go."

Up to this point Lisa had been very polite but the laughter broke the ice for both of us. We were now on the same page and were not afraid to be ourselves. A friendship was developing on that early June Morning as we found the exit and escaped to the city sidewalks with no destination in mind.

The Lisbon Harbor is very much like San Francisco. It is the inside of surrounding land that creates a need for bridges or ferries to get to other towns that are separated by the Tagus River. Lisa and I walked along the edge of the water watching ships and recreational sail boats setting out on their respective destinations.

"Want to take a ferry across and see what's on the other side?" I said.

"Definitely, that would be fun."

I felt responsible for showing her something that would make her visit to Lisbon more memorable than walking through museums. I had not taken the ferry to Almada, located across the river, but I figured it would be a nice adventure for both of us. Our timing could not have been better if we had planned it. We found the location where cars and people were boarding the ferry, bought a ticket and walked across the plank onto the large craft.

What made the crossing special was standing on the deck, feeling the breeze created by the motion of the boat and the natural gust of wind cascading off the water. Watching the city shrink in size as we moved further from Lisbon, I felt a rush of happiness; we were young, we were new friends and we did not have a care in the world. We did not know what was on the other side but did know that whatever it was, it would be good because it was new. When you are young, you take it for granted; youth is not appreciated until you do not have it anymore and why should it be? We are not as wise as we will be, through our lifelong experiences; yet the wisest part of being young is something we often lose when we become older; being fully alive in the moment.

Lisa and I were in the moment that afternoon. There was no intimacy, only friendship as we walked along the harbor of Almada, exploring shops and talking about our lives as we emptied the deeper parts of our individual souls. We found an outdoor fish market with a small restaurant and ate chowder at a wooden table along the waterfront. As we ate, she told me of her failed relationship and broken heart; her life in Boston and the fact that this place we were at now was very much like the Boston Harbor. I told her of dropping out of college and working in a factory in Costa Mesa so I could earn the money for this trip. I held back the story of my own broken heart; my marriage to Carole that lasted only a week. She was so nice, I thought she would be overly sympathetic, and I did not want that to be part of this wonderful day.

Before we left Almada, Lisa mentioned how in Boston, people would often buy Crabs and have a Crab Bake on the beach, so we decided to have our own crab bake of sorts; buying two cooked crabs at one of the fish markets. The day was late when we boarded the ferry for the return to Lisbon with our crabs and some souvenirs Lisa had purchased. Our plan was to have a picnic on the balcony of the Pension so as we walked back from the ferry landing in Lisbon; we bought a loaf of bread and a bottle of Lancer's Wine, a Portuguese wine that was popular in America at that time. I can remember very clearly sitting on the deck of the small balcony, watching the activity of the city one story below as we feasted on Crab, bread and wine. I realized then that Lisa and I could have easily been lovers if circumstances had been different. I liked her very much.

The following day, Sunday, was to be her last in Lisbon as she and Susan were taking an all-night train to Madrid. By this time there was no question that Lisa was going to ditch Susan again when I told her about Estoril. Together we spent another lovely day at the beach that by now was my favorite place to be in Portugal. Later that evening, after returning to the Pension, Lisa, Susan and I walked to the same café we had gone the first night they were in Lisbon. Through the conversation at dinner, Susan, out of the blue, asked me if I had previously been married. It was a subject that I had decided not to discuss with Lisa, but I could not lie so I told them the story of Carole.

When I finished Lisa looked at me, somewhat shocked and said, "You never told me about that." I think she was somewhat hurt because we had shared our souls over the past two days.

"I know," I said. "I just didn't want to ruin our short time together."

Susan spoke, "That must have hurt you very deeply. I could see it in your eyes as you told the story."

They left that night and I wondered which of the two girls had the best memories of Lisbon; Susan who visited the museums or Lisa who spent two days exploring the area with a new friend. I know what I would have chosen. Once again, I was alone with the stirred-up memory of Carole and the essence of the joyful two days with Lisa, mixed feelings to be sure. I never forgot her, even though our encounter was so brief.

Chapter 27

I STAYED ANOTHER four nights in Lisbon, spending most of my days taking the train to Estoril and reading. It was truly a vacation within a vacation but now, it was time to move on. My next destination was Faro, located at the southern tip of Portugal. I really did not know much about Faro but had read about it in one of the Michener Books, which had described it as a nice beach resort. I left Lisbon on a late afternoon train on the 8th of June and arrived in Faro around ten o'clock that night. Walking out of the very small train station, I realized I was on the outskirts of the town and that there were no streetlights to guide me. I had no idea where I was but walked for nearly a mile toward what I thought the town was located. Still not seeing anything that resembled civilization and being tired I decided I would just find a place that I could sleep that would be safe. Continuing toward, I found an empty field, laid my tube tent out for ground cover, unrolled my sleeping bag and crawled in with my clothes on. It never occurred to me that there was danger. I did have some nervousness that a policeman or owner of the property would roust me, but not that anyone would rob or kill me. That kind of thinking was just not on my radar.

I woke with the sun after only a few hours of sleep, tired, sore and hungry. I realized that I was not that far from the town; I just could not tell because the town was not well lit the night before. Of course, any time I could save on a nights lodging was a bonus. At that time, Faro was a small town with really nothing to keep me there but the beaches which were located on a peninsula called Ancao and on an island named Deserta. I located the ferry that was going to one of the locations and ended up on a very deserted beach with just a few shops and a hotel restaurant called Carousel. The hotel looked a bit out of my price range, which was next to zero anyway, so I walked about a half mile to a deserted part of the beach and set up camp for the next three days.

I had been alone many times already on this trip, but this was like Robinson Crusoe lonely. There was no one around and for those three days, the only company was the staff at the Carousel, where I would walk twice a day; once for breakfast and to buy water and food to make my lunch and then back to the restaurant each evening, for dinner and wine. My routine allowed me time to swim during the day and star gaze at night. Fortunately, I had my guitar and I continued to read and study my Spanish. It was quite austere, even for a vagabond, but still better than Salamanca because I had a beach.

When I finally packed and took the ferry back to Faro, I must have been quite a sight. The only bathing, I had been exposed to was jumping into the Atlantic for my daily swims. I found a decent hotel that was not expensive and enjoyed a shower and the opportunity to wash my clothes in the bathroom sink. After a good night's sleep, I repacked my backpack; my next destination was Seville, back in Spain. The train was to leave mid-morning, so I had time to eat the breakfast that was provided at the hotel. After eating I set off for the train station, arriving an hour early. I put my pack on the ground, sat beside it on the floor and pulled out the book I was reading. Suddenly I was approached by the proprietor of the hotel who was accompanied by a policeman. They stood above me and in broken English the hotel owner or manager accused me of stealing a towel from my hotel room. They were nice towels, but I did not take one and told him so. The policeman obviously did not believe me and asked me to open my pack, which I did proving I had no towel. The hotel manager was surprised and embarrassed as he realized it must have been one of his staff who took the towel. I may have looked like a hippie by this time in my travels, but I was not a thief.

My original guide for my time in Spain was Michener's Iberia, which I started reading months before embarking on my European adventure. I went to Seville because it was in the book, as I had Salamanca. I had to admit, the city was beautiful and quite charming, with horse drawn carriages as taxies as well as the lovely parks and architecture, but the heart of this city was in its history. My options with money just did not include visits to museums. For the next three days I tried to like Seville, but I was still alone, so my days consisted of walking the city, going to the park and studying Spanish. I often went to my room, located in a less affluent neighborhood, with the sounds of people yelling and babies crying through the very thin walls from the courtyard below. I continued finding comfort in playing my guitar and writing to Christina and my family. I had been picking up mail at the American Express Offices in major cities as planned before I left and looked forward to receiving news from home. My letters to Chris were a chronology of my travels and allowed me to tell someone of my adventures. I had now been in Europe for six weeks and it would be another six weeks before she would arrive.

The next stop on my loose itinerary was Malaga, at the southernmost coast of Spain, it was the major city on the Costa del Sol. Malaga was not in the book *Iberia*, but it was in the Michener Novel, *The Drifters*, which was a much less disciplined read and much more entertaining. The story of young people doing what I was doing, searching for meaning while traveling in Europe. I was quite ready to step away from Iberia and the historical research, which was too much like school. Searching for meaning and my soul was much more to my liking. I had found it in Lisbon, and it was time to find it again. I finally understood that having someone to share experiences, like I had with Aad, Marcus and Lisa was better than being alone. Besides, Michener had written that if a young man could not find a girl in Torremolinos, which was near Malaga, then he was basically a loser. Not that I wanted to find a girl, I had one, Christina, but I wanted to see if I could. So, after three days in Seville, I boarded the train for Malaga.

I liked Malaga immediately and discovered that cities like people had differing personalities and the ones close to the coast had my kind of soul. I had my first octopus' sandwich with a bottle of cold Spanish beer that I thought was wonderful. I ventured to the seaside village of Torremolinos but did not see many available women. But I did run into an American about my age who was from somewhere in the mid-west. He sported a heavy beard and looked like a mountain man just out of the mountains of Colorado. We connected, because that was what happened when you saw another crazy American vagabond who was traveling alone. We soon became friends and spent the next few days in Malaga. We both searched for women and cold bottles of beer; the beer was easily found but the women were not. Perhaps it was because they were in the nightclubs and neither Paul nor I could afford going to them. So, the dream of Torremolinos was a bust but I still liked it better than Seville of Salamanca.

I told Paul I was heading to Barcelona in northern Spain and he decided to join me. It was a long trip from Malaga, so we decided to take an overnight train and save money on lodging. I had just purchased a new book, John Steinbeck's East of Eden and became so absorbed in it that I spent the whole night sitting on the floor between train cars, because there was light and read the book.

Barcelona, I discovered, was a big city; the biggest I had visited in Spain, and I fell in love with it. The port with the statue of Christopher Columbus, the Gaudi Architecture and the Ramblas were all part of the character of Barcelona. We found a student hostel in the upper end of Barcelona and walked every day to the port as we took in the sight, sounds and aroma of this vibrant Spanish City. It would be 31 years before I returned to Barcelona to re-discover the architecture and heart of the city that did not change but the character did change. I knew from my reading that Francisco Franco, General of the Nationalists during the Spanish Civil War, became the ruler and dictator of Spain after his victory in 1939. His tyrannical influence was still part of Spain's culture until he died in 1975 and with his death, Barcelona became a much more cosmopolitan city. But in 1972, there were still restrictions on how people dressed and what books and postcards were displayed in shops around the city.

On Sunday, the 25th of June, Paul informed me he was out of money and had asked his parents to wire him more. He asked to borrow some money that he would pay back when he got it from home.

"How are you going to find me?" I said.

"You are going to Pamplona for the running of the bulls, aren't you?" He asked.

"Yes".

"That is in July, I plan to be there too. Let's meet somewhere at a designated time and place and I can pay you back."

I was skeptical and hated to part with the money but he was a travel brother and so we agreed to meet at Castle Square on July 6th at two different times; noon and/or 5 p.m. I then gave him $20 and we said goodbye until we would meet in Pamplona.

I had already decided, after looking at travel posters in the various travel agencies of Barcelona that I was going to go to the island of Ibiza. There was really no reason for me to go, it was not on my planned itinerary, but I was ahead of schedule and it looked like a cool place. I boarded an all-night ship that left from the port of Barcelona, traveling economy class that offered seats which reclined to allow people to sleep during the voyage, but as I walked around the deck, I realized I could spread my sleeping bag out under a lifeboat and watch the stars. I had no idea, as I drifted off to sleep, that what lay before me was to be a pivotal highpoint of my trip that would change the character of the rest of my travels as well as, in many ways my life.

Chapter 28

I WOKE WITH the first light of dawn and sounds of people walking by the lifeboat that served as my roof during the night. We were approaching the port of Ibiza and many of the passengers were just beginning to move around to watch the island as we approached. I looked at the blue-black sky and noticed there were no clouds; it would be a beautiful summer day on this next adventure. The sun was just rising out of the distant backdrop of a village on a hill; I could not wait to discover what lay before me; I had no idea what to expect but as always, I was curious.

Before disembarking, I bought a roll and a cup of coffee and wondered where I would stay; I really did not want to spend money on a hotel. When I traveled with Jerry in 1969 it seemed that we saw a lot of campgrounds, but then we had a car. I was on foot and so far, almost two months into this trip, I had not visited one campground. So, when I left Barcelona, I decided that I would seek out a campground. As I walked toward the city that morning, I came to a crossroad with the familiar campground sign pointing away from Ibiza town with 5 Km displayed. Well that must be a good sign, I thought; about 3 miles, I can walk that.

I recall very clearly the walk that took me about an hour and a half along a dirt walkway with tufts of dead yellow grass bordering the paved two-lane street. In 1972 Ibiza was a fairly new tourist attraction and most people stayed in the port city. As I walked, I saw another sign for San Antoni which was a bit further than the campground, and would later discover, was a growing city on the other side of the island. There were few cars on the road as I walked with my pack and guitar, so hitchhiking was not a good option. But I enjoyed the beautiful morning and the freedom to just appreciate the dry countryside and intermittent houses along the road. I eventually arrived at a spot that had much more greenery, with plants and trees, and the arrow sign with the camping insignia pointing down a paved road about 50 yards. This would be my home for the next week. As I approached the office to see about a space, I noticed a camp store and a swimming pool. This was a pretty cool place, I thought.

There were not many camper vans, nothing like you see in today's campgrounds in America with the huge houses on wheels. Here were mostly tents and a few mini vans. There was no one who was camping like me. I went to my designated spot after checking in. I thought the couple that worked the campground wondered why this crazy American was checking in without a vehicle or tent; but I would soon learn, I was not the only person to do so.

The spot I was assigned to was in an area away from other campers, which was fine by me. It was the size of a single car garage; all grass and behind me the road coming into the campground that was lined by cypress trees. I spread my plastic tent on the grass, unrolled my sleeping bag and set my pack and guitar on top. I was still always careful to keep my passport and traveler's checks in my boot; I could handle it if anything else was stolen but not those items. I then went back to the camp store to buy French style bread, cheese and salami and a tomato for my lunch. It was such a beautiful day and since there were no campers near my space, I ate my lunch and then began to play the guitar, quite content with myself and life at that moment.

I had been playing for a while when a gray English style van rolled by me and stopped about three spaces to my right as I faced the little road. On the back of the van was a drawing of a mouse sporting an oversized member of its anatomy and the words; Boerie Tours. I stopped playing as I watched five young guys with long hair like mine step out of the van stretching and laughing; apparently having fun as they began to erect a small tent; a real tent.

I went back to playing and singing softly so I would not draw attention to myself but the sight of a young man sitting alone and playing a guitar was too curious for a couple of them and two strolled over to my site and listened as I played. Both were tall like me; one had blond curly hair and dark horned rim glasses and the other, long auburn hair and thick mutton chops.

"Can you play any Cat Stevens," the blond one said with a British accent.

"No," I said. "I like his music, but never tried to play it. Most of my music is old folk and my own that I wrote."

"You're American?" the darker haired one asked.

"Yeah," I answered, then asked "you too?"

"No, Canadian. My name is Jay" he said, then pointed to his friend, "this is Trevor, he is from South Africa."

I would soon learn that the group consisted of three Canadians and three South Africans who were traveling in two vans. They had met each other a couple of weeks before at a campground in Southern Spain. The other van was with one of the South Africans, who stayed in Barcelona because he had met a girl. He would be arriving later, or they would meet up with him in Barcelona before heading to Pamplona for San Fermin.

Trevor, asked me to play something and so I did, a bit embarrassed but thought, what the hell. As I played the other three, who had finished their task of putting up the tent, walked over to listen. After one song, I put my guitar down and stood up, introducing myself. The other three did the same. There was Brian and Paul who like Jay was from Richmond, British Columbia, and Michael who along with Trevor had traveled from Durban, South Africa. Immediately we all became friends and would be inseparable for the next two weeks.

For the rest of the day we got to know each other, sharing tales of our travel, swimming in the pool and enjoying the day. Then as evening approached the six of us decided to go into town, about a mile walk, to find a good Paella for dinner. Wandering through the narrow streets of the town I thought was Sant Antoni but was actually a village a bit further south called Sant Josep, we avoided the nicer restaurants catering to tourists. We wanted to find something where locals would go, finally locating a small restaurant with the name "Bambi", that really was part of someone's home; more like an apartment that a storefront.

We all entered the small dining room and found a large wood table with a plastic table cover that would accommodate the six of us. It appeared that a young couple, with two small children, were the owners. I asked the man, in my limited Spanish if they had Paella. He explained in very broken English that the Paella would take a few hours to prepare. If we would come back tomorrow and they knew how many, we could have it made special for us. We ended up ordering off a small menu and made a pact to come back the following evening.

After dinner, we walked the streets for a while before heading back to the campground. As we walked, Jay mentioned that there was a place down the street that that rented Mopeds. They were planning on checking it out the next day and asked if I would like to join them. The Africans were not going to spend any unnecessary money, but I decided, I would splurge; it sounded fun.

Before the night ended, we had a nightcap beer outside the camp store. Two young ladies that we had not seen before came up to the store and we all introduced ourselves. The girls were from New York; one a short and quite pretty with longish raven hair, named Ronda and her friend Charlotte who was more tomboyish and shy. They would be an addition to our group that grew with each passing day.

When you are 24, you can sleep, night after night on the hard ground. You wake up sore but in a very short time after walking to the public bathroom and having a cigarette and coffee from the camp store while enjoying the morning air, the soreness becomes a distant memory. I was looking forward to renting motorbikes with the Canadians. Soon they all found their way to the store where I was sitting, and we ate rolls with butter and jam for breakfast.

After eating the three Canadians and I walked to the motor bike rentals and chose mopeds to take around the island. We did not have to wear helmets and were free to go wherever we wanted. It was a slice of heaven as we motored like some small-time motorcycle gang; the weather in late June magnificent as we traveled from one end of the island to the other. Ibiza is about 25 miles long and half that wide. We went from Sant Josep, where we started; up to the port of Sant Antoni that was a bigger city but still small in 1972. It is impossible to recall the entire day and details of our adventure. I can only imagine, though, how fun it was with my new friends, all of us in our early twenties, exploring this Balearic Island off the Mediterranean Coast of Spain; the sun warming us against the breeze as we each took in the beauty of the countryside and surrounding sea. There were two very distinct occurrences on that ride though that I do remember vividly.

We had been riding for a couple of hours when we arrived at the town of Ibiza, where I had first arrived only a day before. Since the town is built on a hill we were planning on parking and walking up to explore but before we got off our bikes, Ronda and Charlotte walked up to us with a new girl I had not met before. She was not a girl, but a beautiful woman, I would learn later of 30. Debby introduced her to us as we sat on our mopeds. Her name was Cari and she was on holiday from London. As we met, something happened; a look perhaps, maybe a smile or the look in her eyes, but there was a chemistry I could not explain, and the memory of her stayed with me throughout the day. We chatted with these ladies for a while then they left and we walked up to the town to have some lunch. We found a place that was very American, and I ordered a hamburger, which I had not had since leaving Amsterdam. I was in heaven.

After lunch we carried on exploring the island and after another hour arrived back to Sant Josep. As we rounded a corner we came upon a café and spotted Trevor and Michae sitting at a wooden table having a beer. We parked our bikes and walked over to say hi and they suggested we take our bikes back to the rental spot and come back to join them, which is what we did.

By the time we walked back, there were two new guys sitting with the South Africans who would become new members of our group; Ken, who had red hair and beard, and Dan, a burly, dark haired young man, who looked like a football linebacker. Ken, who was from New Jersey, would later be named Ginger Beard by a young boy who was with his parents from England staying at the campground; the name stuck, although we called him GB for short. Dan, though a bruiser looking young man, turned out to be a gentle giant with a very sweet disposition.

We ordered beers now eight of us sitting around the table and talked of our individual lives back home. Trevor and Michael traveling from Durbin had gone to school together, becoming friends playing Rugby. Michael, who was shorter and stout, looked like you would expect a Rugby player to look. Trevor, who was my height, was the romantic of the two. He loved music and musicals and loved the idea of being in love. Both the Africans mentioned that Ronda and Charlotte had come back to the campground earlier and said they had seen us at the port. Trevor told me later that he liked Ronda and hoped to get involved with her while in Ibiza. He also mentioned that the lady Cari seemed interested in me.

"Ronda said she fancies you," he said.

That was nice but I did have a girlfriend. Still the idea of a romance in Ibiza was intriguing and I was attracted to her after our meeting earlier that day.

During the day, I had become better acquainted with the Canadians. Jay, the auburn haired one, was a prankster and the most outgoing. Brian was an English gentleman with a strong British accent since his parents had immigrated to Canada when he was in middle school. Paul was shyer and quieter; he had a deep voice and blushed crimson very easily. He along with Trevor would become good friends with me as the trip that summer progressed, probably because we were most alike.

We continued to order more beers, a party had definitely started, and as the day grew into late afternoon, the bottles accumulated on the table. A waiter tried to take them away, but we decided to keep them there, for no other reason than to show anyone who cared to notice, we were having a party. I don't know how many beers I had at that point, but I know we were having a great time. Of course, drinking beer in quantities requires more frequent stops to the WC. Trevor and I both left the table to take turns in the café's bathroom. We began talking and he told me of his lost love in Durban who ended up marrying someone else. He and Michael had been traveling for several months, originally going to London where they each got jobs to support this summer trip around the continent. I told him about Carole and Christina, my work in the factory that allowed me to get to Europe. We had a lot in common both in life and perspective.

Back at the table the beer continued to flow which made conversation more philosophical with subjects running deep on such subjects as sports, travel and women. Suddenly our waiter came to the table to explain that the distributer from a local rival beer company said if we allowed the tables, (now two), to be cleared of our accumulated bottles, they would buy us all a beer with their brand. I believe we negotiated with Michael as our spokesman who had by this time enough to drink to be bold enough to say we would do it if we could have two beers each. It was agreed and since all of us vagabonds were on a limited budget it was also appreciated.

By the time we finished those last beers it was getting dark and we agreed it was time to go to the Bambi restaurant for our special Paella. We must have been quite a sight as six of us drunken young men navigated through the narrow streets, talking loud as drunks do and singing. It was all harmless until Michael got into an argument with a couple of Spanish young men and we had to pull him back before it got out of hand.

Arriving at Bambi, the young couple was quite happy, although we were a bit loud, they did not seem to mind. As planned earlier, Rhonda and Charlotte joined the group. I looked for Cari, but she was not with them. Trevor made a point of sitting with Ronda as we sat down for our feast of freshly baked Paella. This day had been a scene right out of some movie from the beginning to this dinner as we reveled together with good food and cheap wine. I could not have been happier. These people, my age, with the same adventurous soul as I had forged a bond in the past two days that was remarkable. If I had a day, I could relive it would be this day. If I had a week, it would be this week in Ibiza.

For the next two days, the last days of June, we all cut back on our drinking, mostly to save money more than for health reasons. We continued to be regulars at the Bambi Restaurant because the food was good and inexpensive, and I think the young couple adopted us hooligans. Clive Peterson made his arrival with his girlfriend Kelly. Clive was the third of this South African trio who had remained in Barcelona with his American girlfriend. Together they pulled into the campground in the African's red Volkswagen van that the trio had shared while traveling around Europe. He was tall and thin, looked a bit like the young Rod Stewart and had a very charming personality. A born businessman, he always figured the angles telling us stories of turning in his camera a couple of times as stolen to the insurance company to receive reimbursement. He also was famous with the South Africans for selling admission to soccer matches in Durban by sneaking friends through the exit.

Our days were lazy and fun as the group became closer spending time at the campground pool or walking into town as June slipped into July. That was the day, July first that I ran into Cari again. It was in the lobby of the hotel she was staying, on a Saturday evening. The group had decided to meet there and then go to a nightclub that one of the girls had heard about from Cari. As we sat in the lobby, waiting for everyone to show up, by this time 12 of us, someone had a guitar, so Trevor suggested I play a couple of songs. I typically did not like playing for others especially a growing crowd in the hotel lobby, but on this night, for some reason, I felt confident and played. It was one of those magical nights where my soul shined through the person I normally lived with. Perhaps I was caught up in the energy of Ibiza and the people that now formed a group of in-crowd young people having fun in a foreign country; whatever it was, I was on.

After I played, we all moved out of the lobby and down the narrow street as easily as a group of nearly a dozen could; with conversations and laughter echoing off the buildings as we headed toward the nightclub. As I walked, Cari was at my side; coincidence or planned I don't know but certainly a pleasure for me. With my personality stronger than normal, we talked about the group and about her and about me and I found myself falling for this pretty blond woman five years older than me.

Without paying attention to where we were or how long we walked, we suddenly were at our destination. The nightclub was a disco, like so many in Europe; dark, loud and crowded, and for me none of it mattered. I don't think we ever sat down because there was no place to sit. Somehow, we managed to get drinks and we stood in the crowd trying to talk through the blast of music that pulsated throughout the bar. Cari never left my side; the others were there but as far as I was concerned, we were alone as I became intoxicated with alcohol and this lovely English lady. For perhaps a couple of hours we talked, danced and then kissed. Then she asked if I would walk her back to her hotel, which I did and then ended up in her room where we had wild, drunk sex into the wee hours.

After very little sleep Cari woke me to inform me, I had to leave early because the hotel had a rule of no one staying who was not a paying customer. So, we made love again and I snuck out through the back stairs before it got light. I was smiling to myself, thinking of the craziness of what happened and me having to sneak out. As I walked back to the campground, I thought of this very interesting lady. She was 30, I was 8 days away from being 25. She worked in London in her own shop, making silver jewelry; successful enough to take holidays like this one that had brought her to Ibiza. She was recently divorced, had no children and was set to depart for London the next day.

I thought of Chris with a tinge of guilt. We never said we would not see other people, but to me it was understood, it was not encouraged. I walked into the campground and Michael was the only one up. He saw me as a walked toward him and said, "where were you?"

"I slept in town."

"With Cari?" He said.

"Yeah."

He smiled and said "Oww, Andy got a haircut." I smiled too. Even though I really liked Cari, there was the badge of honor for scoring the prettiest and most desirable of the available women. I had elevated to a new level and with Michael, who was one of the leaders, this American from California was pretty cool.

It was Sunday, July 2nd and the trip to Ibiza was coming to an end. The boys were planning on leaving the island on the 4th of July and traveling to Pamplona and the running of the bulls, San Fermin Festival. I had been invited to go with them and looked forward to the experience, but on this day, it was Cari's last full day, so I decided to spend it with her. I showered, changed clothes and went back to her hotel to meet in the lobby as we had planned. We immersed ourselves in the day, walking, talking, and eating Tapas with coffee. Conversations turned from getting to know each other better to an invitation for me to go to London during my travels and staying with her. It reminded me of the morning with Marta in Amsterdam three years before and how I wanted to do that with her. I could get a job in London and live with this beautiful lady, but Christina was coming at the end of July and I could not let her down.

There was a bit of fallout because of my romance with Cari. Ken, "GB", was upset. He had a huge crush on Cari and was a bit broken hearted. That last night, I once again stayed with her. She had an early flight the following morning, but we still stayed up talking. She gave me a silver star on a chain that she had made and wrote her address in my pocket calendar. When dawn broke, I snuck out of the hotel and back to the campground. I never saw her again but heard over the next couple of months that GB also got her address and he did stay with her. His adventure turned positive after all.

Trevor and Ronda were now an item; he was sleeping in her tent, but that too was coming to an end as they traveled in different directions that summer. Trevor being the one who kept in touch with everyone never lost touch with her. We had a farewell party at Bambi's the night of July 3rd for one last Paella. The next morning, the fourth of July, we slowly packed the vans and killed time before caravanning to Ibiza for the night crossing to Barcelona. I recall after we had parked the vans on the ship, Trevor and I walked up to the deck to watch the sun set. Looking out across the water toward Sant Josep, as the ship launched, Trevor began singing the soundtrack to Camelot. I listened as my mind thought of Cari, the 4th of July in America and the leaving Ibiza, definitely the best week of my time in Europe. Of course, there were still many adventures that lay ahead.

Chapter 29

AS I HAVE mentioned, travel is a great metaphor for life. Drawing on Joseph Campbell's philosophy of the *Hero's Journey*, *"we must go to the unknown and follow our "Bliss", which lies in our intuitive conscious soul to find the unexpected"*. I don't know why I went to Ibiza. It was not on my plan; I just wanted to go to one of the Baleric Islands while I had a chance. As I walked along the two-lane road, I never could have dreamed the experience that would change the course of my travels that summer. The friends, the wonderful days and nights of fun and shared adventures, and even the brief love affair with Cari which, as it turned out, saved the relationship Chris and I were to have were all the result of going into the unknown and intuition.

The ferry from Ibiza arrived in Barcelona early Wednesday morning on the 5th of July. My plan now, was to ride in one of the vans to Pamplona. The San Fermin, running of the bulls was 2 days away. We spent the morning on the steps of the main post office near the harbor waiting for it to open so the boys could check their mail. As I sat there, I watched the early morning bustle of this amazing city. I did not know it then, but of all the cities I would visit in the world, Barcelona would be my favorite. There is something very special about this city that is hard to put into words. It is perhaps the Spanish Culture and the charm of the Ramblas, and the Gaudi Architecture. It would be another thirty years before I came back but the memory would stay with me beckoning me to return.

We left for Pamplona sometime before noon after stocking up on staples of bread, cheese, salami, ham, tomatoes, onions and water. The two vans caravanned west. I traveled with the Canadians while the South Africans along with the American girl, Kelly traveled in the red Volkswagen van. It is about 300 miles from Barcelona to Pamplona and it took the better part of the day to make the journey; stopping along the way for a mid-day meal and break. By the time we arrived in Pamplona it was evening, so we proceeded to a camp ground first, before going into town. Finding a campground was more difficult than we anticipated as many were already full because of the festival. We did finally find one in the hills that surrounded the city a few miles away; not walking distance but since we had vehicles it would do. We purchased two sites and created a small compound with the vans, tents and me sleeping on the ground in the open air. I preferred the openness of watching the stars before falling asleep. Certainly, it was better than sleeping in a van with a bunch of guys.

San Fermin begins each year at noon on July 6th with evening festivities and fireworks until midnight. The running of the bulls begins the following morning on the 7th of July. The morning of the 6th, we drove into town to explore; I also had a date to meet Paul at Castle Square and get my Twenty Dollars back. Since I had been there earlier in May, I showed the boys Castle Square, some of the bars and where the bull ring was located. We all decided that sometime during the festival we would go to a bullfight. I planned to go on my birthday, two days into the festival. I also decided I was not going to run with the bulls, but instead, just be a spectator. It was tempting for sure, but every year it seemed someone got hurt or killed on the run and I just wasn't up for that kind of danger. As it turned out, Paul never showed. I was disappointed because of the money but figured he either had to return to the US or just could not make it to Pamplona for the festival. I wrote it off as helping a travel brother and besides, meeting the group not only had enhanced my experience, I had saved money by sharing travel expenses. It was a fair balance.

The next day, July 7th, we woke early, went into town to find a place to watch the first day of the running of the bulls. We parked outside the city and walked into town to find the streets lined with wooden barricades creating a path from outside Pamplona near the Arga River, through the streets for a half mile to the Plaza de Torres, (Bull Ring). The early morning air enhanced my senses as I looked at all the people lined along the barricades. There were certainly more watchers than runners; wise souls, I thought.

We found a spot to watch about halfway from Castle Square and the Bull Ring. Trevor, Michae and the Canadians; Brian, Jay and Paul all found spaces to squeeze in so we could see the craziness of grown men running down a narrow street with bulls chasing them. Clive had decided to run and had gone into town separate from us. Suddenly we could hear the commotion from spectators up the street as the runners and bulls approached. There they were a large group of men and six or seven huge bulls both behind and amongst them. Some of the runners, to avoid being run down, slipped into doorways and others dove under the barricades to be out of the lane of these ferocious beasts that were both confused and angry as they slashed the air with their horns. We looked for Clive but did not see him. I wondered if he had ducked away before he got to us but learned later he had jumped in the lane, near the bull ring and went inside the arena with the group of runners and the bulls that would die that day individually as each bull fight took place.

It was all great fun getting caught up in the festivity of this ritual, but certainly not anything an animal rights person would approve of. Since San Fermin, formerly, Los Sanfermines is a weeklong, our adventure had just begun. Pamplona is in the northern Basque Region of Spain and true to tradition the men dress in white linen shirts and trousers, and sport red scarfs and red berets. Throughout the week it is a total party atmosphere and for a group of young guys who liked to drink, it was another holiday within a vacation. A couple of the boys purchased Bota bags to drink their wine, another Basque tradition and for the most part, we behaved ourselves; just once did we have a scuffle with a group of Spanish young men, but we ended up shaking hands and sharing some wine from one of the Bota bags I have always been a fan of working it out.

On the morning of my 25th Birthday, I woke before anyone else and hiked up into the hills that surrounded the campground. I took the small note tablet I had been keeping notes in and a pen, found a place to sit with a view of the rocky terrain of Northern Spain, and began to write my reflections of what it felt like to be 25. I have kept that essay of my philosophy at that point in my life and shared it with my daughters when they each turned 25. It is interesting to read now at this time in my life because I do believe I was in many ways wiser than, than later in my life when I decided to chase money and success. There was a point where I came to understand who I was, and a philosophy born out of the last five years of the experiences I have written in this memoir. It had nothing to do with school but more about pursuing the dreams of my soul. At some point over those years I had discovered a freedom that I later lost, under the guise of responsible living, but have drawn on that feeling at times, to find my true self. At my core, I still seek the freedom, adventure and the love of life. All the money, power and position does not and cannot replace the inner core of one's soul. As I have mentioned in this memoir, I was perpetually conflicted with desire against duty. For the time being, while in Europe, I was living out my desire.

Finishing the three-page essay, I walked back to our campsite, excited about the day. On the agenda was calling home to talk to my family and Christina. Because of the nine-hour time difference I planned on calling around 5 pm which would be 8 am in California. Before that, we were going to go to the bull fight. We had seen enough of the running of the bulls to not feel the need to go every day, so on that morning we hung out at the campground and had breakfast.

My friendship with Trevor was deepening, as it was with his sidekick Michael and the Canadian Paul. I believe it was the four of us that went to the bullfights that day. I can still recall sitting in the stands of the circular arena watching the pageantry; the people having fun as if at a Sunday afternoon football game in America. Only on this Sunday afternoon it was the matadors facing down six bulls, one event at a time; dancing around the angry, charging beasts with a flare and individual style, each unique, yet each with the same process; the bull always died. It is an art; a skilled sport and it is cruel. Even as I watched that day, my feelings for these beautiful and brave animals made me not ever want to go to another bullfight again. Still, I was not going to ruin my day with righteous indignation. I continued to enjoy the moment and the experience.

The afternoon wore on and we stayed for the entire event, with the blazing Spanish sun keeping us uncomfortably warm as each bull was one by one drug off the bloody dirt arena as conquered gladiators. After it was all over and we moved with the crowd to the streets outside, I separated from the boys to find the communications office that would allow me to place a call home.

In 1972, telephoning the U.S from Spain, was a difficult process. Not only was there the time difference, but you had to have an operator at a special location that offered that service. It was now Sunday Morning in Fresno and I wondered if Chris would be there. There had not been mail from her in a couple of weeks as I checked the American Express offices in both Barcelona and Pamplona. I wondered if she had changed her mind or lost enthusiasm over Europe or me. But on that day, she was there when I connected to my parents' phone. We talked briefly, there was not a lot of time to waste; she said she would meet me in Amsterdam at the end of the month, which was almost two weeks. When I asked why she had not written recently, she explained that she had been busy with school and work. I then talked to my mom, dad and sisters; superficial stuff, how are you what is it like in Europe? It was good to hear from everyone, I missed home, but now I was having the time of my life; so different from all those lonely days and nights while traveling alone.

That evening, back at the campground we had a celebration for two birthdays. Trevor's birthday was July 10th. To this day, we never miss calling each other for our birthdays. He usually calls me because my day comes first and if he misses me, he leaves a message and then I call back the next day and we invariably talk about the evening in Pamplona in 1972, singing by a campfire with all the friends we had made in Ibiza that had caravanned to Pamplona. I had my guitar and Trevor was using some pots and pans for a drum as we sang "Summertime" from Porgy & Bess. It was an amazing birthday, an amazing time in my life and as I write about it now, I can still feel the joyous emotions of that time.

We left Pamplona two days later and went into the mountains to Andorra, a small country nestled in the Pyrenees Mountains between Spain and France. We needed a few days to escape the wild party of San Fermin. I came down with a cold and hung low as we discussed our individual plans. I was going to head north to Amsterdam to meet Christina; the boys were heading for the Mediterranean Coast of France. It was July 15th when they dropped me off at a train station in Narbonne France. Our plan was to meet in Munich at the Octoberfest toward the end of September. Of course, that would change as the adventure continued for all of us, but at that moment, it was goodbye. I was alone again and would remain that way, with one brief exception until I met Chris at Schiphol Airport, two days before her 19th birthday on July 26.

Chapter 30

I STEPPED OFF the train in Paris as the early morning light of dawn brought a new day to this incredible city. Since Narbonne is on the cusp of the Mediterranean Sea, the train to Paris was an all-night trip which allowed me another opportunity to save on a night's lodging. I had a week before Christina was to arrive at Schiphol, so I decided to spend a few more days in Paris, taking in the city sights, sounds and aromas that is surely its own unique character. It is always interesting to me how decisions can change the course of the journey and this one was no exception.

As usual, I had no idea where I was going to stay but, I had discovered that was just part of the game. It had been two months since I was here last but could not find where I had stayed before so I had to find a new hostel that was cheap and still close to the main attractions of the city. I must have walked for two hours that day before a young man who appeared Arabic approached me and asked a question in French.

"I only speak English," I said.

His eyes, widened without smiling, "No English".

Amazingly, without much verbal communication we created a brief friendship over the next 24 hours. It turned out he knew some English and somehow communicated that he had just arrived in the city that morning also and was looking for a hostel. Since our objective was the same, the two unlikely companions of the moment began walking together. His name was Mohammad and I never figured out where he was from, possibly Syria or Jordan but a long way from home to be sure. The irony was not lost on me, that once again two souls connected out of both necessity and desire to share the experience. We continued to walk, not talking but communicating by pointing out a common sight such as the river Sein or the Eifel Tower in the distance, and just nodding our heads.

Eventually we found an inexpensive hotel, large and ominous; obviously old with ceilings nearly 18 feet in height that looked like it could have housed Napoleon at one time. It was very similar to the hotel I stayed in my first night when I first arrived in Paris in May. There was a room available with two beds upstairs for a very reasonable rate. Once we dropped of our cargo, we set out to find something to eat. By this time, it was late afternoon and as we walked, we passed what appeared to be a University, though I don't know which one. I do remember we found an Indian Restaurant and ate Rice and Curry as we watched the students that were not much younger than me walking along the boulevard. Somehow Mohammad communicated to me, somewhat irritably; but that was his personality, being irritable; that the girls kept staring at me. He wondered why I did not smile or talk to them. What was strange is, as much as I loved women, I did not see what he did. This was a lesson that would take many years for me to figure out. My own self-image did not believe that women might be attracted to me. I was a contrast of the risk-taking adventurer who was shy around pretty women.

Mohammad and I strolled along the West side of the Seine as darkness fell and finally, both of us exhausted, walked back to the hotel and climbed the stairs to our room. It never occurred to me, that I not only did not really know my roommate but that he could steal my money at night while I slept. As I lay down after taking off my jeans and t-shirt, I had the thought of, "am I safe here?" Of course, looking back, he may have had the same thoughts as he turned out the light and got into his bed. There were no words spoken; we did not understand each other so we laid in silence in the dark with only a slight bit of light streaming in through the curtains from the lights outside. My legs ached from walking all day and suddenly as I stretched them one of my calf muscles cramped; a Charly-horse. I let out a yelp from the pain as I jumped out of bed in an attempt to keep the cramp from knotting up more than it already was. As soon as I hit the floor, throwing my blanket aside, Mohammad let out a scream of his own as he, probably having the same safety concerns about me thought I was attacking him. When he let out his cry of fear, of course, it startled me, and I jumped back into my own bed, my heart racing. Then, dead quiet as both of us tried to grasp what was happening. As we lay in the quiet for about a minute, I heard Mohammad for the first time that day begin to laugh. It was a low, slow laugh that he was trying to stifle but could not. The sound of his laughter made me realize the humor in what had just happened, and I began to laugh myself. Here we were, two strangers from opposite worlds, different both physically and culturally, laying in this Paris hotel room laughing in the dark.

In the morning Mohammad and I went our separate ways. The inability to communicate and his somewhat sour demeanor made me prefer to be alone. I had been thinking about that scene I had witnessed by the American Express office when I was in Paris in May. I was curious if there still were young people selling used cars. I had begun to consider the possibility of buying a car before Chris arrived. It dawned on me that it would be better and perhaps cheaper than purchasing two train tickets for the remaining two or three months. Then, when we were ready to leave, we could sell the car and have money to stay a while longer. This made very good sense to me; the only fear I had was parting with the money I had for the rest of the trip. It was a gamble. I knew Chris was bringing money for her share so maybe it could work. I looked at the prices listed on the windshields of the cars with sloppy scrawled numbers in American Dollars; $300 to $1,000. No, I could not do this. Running out of money meant the end of the trip; that money was my security. I decided to think about it for another day.

Like buying my guitar in Pamplona, I was conflicted with what to do for the next 24 hours. I went back to the American Express Office to check my mail the next day. I had expected to get one more letter from Chris explaining her excitement of arriving in Europe in just a few more days, but there was nothing. I wondered if she was having second thoughts. What if I bought a car and she did not arrive? Then, the purchase would be silly. Walking out of the Amex Office, my thoughts turned to the cars for sale. I passed by a blue VW bug that looked to be in good shape. A man of about thirty-something standing by the Volkswagen began talking to me as I looked it over. I remember he had shiny black hair combed back into a ponytail. He spoke with a French accent and was what I would call a natural salesperson. I asked him how much for the car; there was no sign. He threw out a a number like five hundred American Dollars. I shook my head and said "no, I can't do that" and began to walk away.

Before I got two steps away, he said, "so what can you do?"

I turned around and said, "No more than three hundred".

He came back with a number in between, like four hundred and I said no and again began to walk.

"Ok, three hundred," he called to me before I got out of hearing range.

I walked back, and he explained, "If I sell this to you for three hundred, you will still have to pay for registration and insurance. That will be another fifty dollars."

I hesitated, that was half of what I had, it was scary but then I thought, Chris and I could have a lot of fun driving around Europe for the rest of the summer. My heart was in my throat as I said, "Ok."

"Great, let me show you where we register."

I followed him to a nearby office building where we climbed the stairs to a second story office. It occurred to me that this was not some traveler, and this was not his first rodeo, as he introduced me to a man behind a desk by his first name, Alfonso. As I look back on the experience I wonder if they were really registering me and provided me insurance or were just trying to make a few more dollars. It was obvious they did this all the time. What did not occur to me was, where did they get their inventory? I would later find out, but for the moment it looked very official as I got the keys, the registration and insurance and handed over my $350.

As I got in the car, I realized that I had no idea if it was running well or not; I had gone on faith and that was typical of me. Fortunately, the VW started right up and now the next challenge; I had not driven a car for nearly three months, and this was Paris, with some of the craziest traffic in the world. I pulled out to the street with the intention of going back to the hostel I had stayed in the previous night. Instead, I ended up in a river of traffic that moved me defensively along major arteries with insane French drivers honking and weaving in and out of lanes. At one point I stopped at a light close to a curb and a bus decided to move into my spot. It did not look like I was in a bus only lane or bus stop so I thought surely the driver sees me and will yield. He did not. Whether he saw me or not, he moved the bus into my car, scratching the driver's door and I think he would have moved me on to the sidewalk had I not pulled forward regardless of the red light. This was a whole new adventure. It took over an hour to get back to the hotel, which was longer than it would have taken me to walk. But I had a car and somehow, I found a place to park, something that was also a challenge in the cities. Now what? I would spend one more night in Paris, then drive to Amsterdam. It was still nearly a week before Chris would arrive, but I was tired of Paris and liked Amsterdam more. I decided to leave the following morning.

The drive was uneventful once I found the right street and then the expressway leading me out of Paris. I avoided the pay roads as much as possible and found the non-pay longer but adequate; I was in no hurry. There were only two border crossings, Belgium which went fine and then the Netherlands. The car was originally registered to the Netherlands and to my good fortune I passed through easily. I would discover later how fortunate I was. In Belgium, I had avoided the large cities of Brussels and Antwerp, so I would not have to navigate traffic. The drive took me most of the day and I was enjoying the freedom I had, now with my own car.

As I approached the city of Amsterdam, I thought about my adventure leaving here the first week nearly three months before. It was now almost 5:00 PM which meant I would be caught in commuter traffic as I entered the city. For the most part, though, the heavy traffic was going out of the city and so in my direction it was not too bad. Suddenly, as I waited at a signal, the VW died. I tried to re-start it but could not. Great; stuck in traffic in Amsterdam, I had no clue what to do except to get out and push the car to the shoulder while holding on to the steering wheel. As I did, I noticed a man pushing behind the car.

He had pulled his car over and jumped out to help me. This is what I loved about Holland; people were friendly, and they spoke English; I was grateful this happened here and not in France. We managed to get the car to the side of the road and when he discovered I only spoke English, told me there was a garage about a half kilometer down the road. "Get in and steer, I will push you with my car."

Fortunately, the garage was still open. The mechanic who was working there told me he was about to close and that if I left my car overnight, he would get to it in the morning. He gave me a phone number and I had to figure out how to get to the city; I had no idea where I was. I told the man that I was headed into town and he told me to walk to the bus stop and take the number 2 bus. I still had Guilders so was able to pay the fare into town. I was not sure where to stay, so I got off the bus and walked in an area that had hotels and found a somewhat inexpensive hostel. I began to worry at this point about money because I had no clue what it would cost to fix the car. Thoughts of what a mistake I had made buying this car penetrated my brain as I tried to sleep that night.

The next day, as it turned out, the part that was replaced was a starter and on the old Volkswagen Bugs it was only a $50-dollar fix. With some relief, I drove off the garage parking lot and back into town to the Hotel Bierenbrodspot to see the ladies with the bed and breakfast and find out if there were any rooms available. They did have a small room in the dormer or attic of their residence, and it was perfect for the next few days until Chris arrived. I concluded that it was too small for both of us as well as the fact, I did not want the ladies to know I would be staying with a woman. Somehow in my mind they seemed too proper for that sort of behavior.

For the balance of the week, while waiting for Chris to arrive, I kept the car parked and walked the streets of Amsterdam. I loved this city; my gateway to Europe that was so friendly and wild at the same time. It was Thursday when I checked in to the Bed & Breakfast and Chris was not to arrive until Monday. I went to the beach in Zandvoort on Friday and just walked and read the balance of the weekend. During those days not only did I anticipate Chris arriving but thought a lot about my experience in Ibiza and Pamplona. I wrote a song about it and since lost the page it was written on, but I do remember the first verse:

> *In the springtime of the season, in the springtime of their lives*
> *They set out for adventure in strange and foreign skies.*
> *And they came up from South Africa, they came from New Jersey*
> *As far as California and Richmond, B.C.*
> *And you know, you'll never grow old.*

On Monday, I checked out of Lotte and Sophie's home and checked in to a nice hotel for Chris and me. By evening, I drove toward Schiphol Airport, wondering if she was even going to show up. I had not heard from her since Pamplona and continued to wondered if she had changed her mind. But as I stood outside the exit for arriving passengers from her flight going through customs, I spotted her. I was both relieved and aware that this adventure was about to change.

Chapter 31

WITH CHRISTINA IN Amsterdam the biggest change was I would no longer be alone. Perhaps the toughest challenge of the first three months was getting used to the loneliness of solitude. Our first night in the hotel I had chosen was a wonderful reunion and I was eager to show her the magical charm of Amsterdam as we got to renew our friendship that had turned into a love affair six months ago but with a three month separation that possibly turned our love affair into a friendship once again. As we walked through the streets of Amsterdam, the first morning. I felt a bit nervous over my brief affair with Cari. I knew I had to tell her but wanted to spend more time that first day before bringing it up. I did not have to wait because she had her own confession to make.

"There is something I need to tell you," she said as we strolled past the train station, heading toward Dam Square. "I spent the weekend with my old boyfriend, Barry over Fourth of July."

At that moment I felt my heart sink into my stomach. The shock on my face must have made her more nervous as she continued. "He lives in Seattle now. He invited me to fly up and see him. I knew it was a mistake, but I don't think I was completely over him after he broke up with me. My mother was furious."

I was blown away. I probably had it coming after Cari, but somehow this seemed more of a betrayal. "I don't understand, how did that happen…getting together again?" I stammered, my head reeling.

"He came to Fresno to see his parents and called me."

"Did you tell him that we were together, that you were meeting me in Europe?" I asked.

"I did, but he didn't care, he told me that he realized he had made a mistake breaking up and wondered if maybe we could try again. I'm sorry Andy, he was very convincing and, well, I hadn't seen you for a while, I wasn't even completely sure we were that secure." She said softly, her eyes tearing up.

"That's why you hadn't written in a month." More of a statement than a question.

"Yes…I'm sorry, I was conflicted."

We came to Dam Square and found a place to sit on the steps of the National Monument. "So. what happened, I mean, you are here; it didn't work out?"

"No," she answered. "Like I said it was a mistake, but he was so sincere, and I knew I had to know."

"So, if it had worked out that weekend you would have not come I suppose."

"I…I don't know. Probably. I needed to know. If I was going to go back with him, I probably wouldn't. By the time I talked to you on your birthday, I knew I didn't want to be with him and was going to see you. I was probably subdued because I was ashamed. When I heard your voice, and you sounded so happy, I knew I wanted to be with you again." She began to cry; a soft tearful sob that she tried to hold back.

I could not help feeling bad for her, but I also was pissed. It felt like such a betrayal. Still, I had my own confession to make but it still hurt like hell. We sat there without speaking for a few minutes. Finally, she said, "are you going to say anything? Do you hate me? You probably wish now I hadn't come."

I measured my response mainly because I wasn't sure what I felt. Anger, hurt, humiliated. It was a groundswell of emotions that I couldn't get hold of. Finally, I said, "no, I don't hate you. I am hurt, I feel a bit betrayed, but I also know I left you for three months and life goes on. I just didn't think you would…" I couldn't find the words. After a moment I said, "I have my own confession."

She looked up at me, her eyes still shiny with tears. "Really?"

I then told her about my week in Ibiza and meeting Cari. As I finished, she seemed almost relieved.

"You know, it is ironic that you were with Barry at the same time I was with her. Kind of strange," I said

"It is. I'm glad you had that experience. Can you forgive me?" She asked.

I didn't answer, I was still in shock. I also was glad I had the experience with Cari. I really don't think I could forgive her if I hadn't. In my mind though, I needed to process all of this. Until I did, I decided to move it to a corner of my mind so as not to ruin our trip. I did not tell her, but something had definitely changed, I could be friends and even lovers for the next two or three months, but I was pretty sure our relationship was not going to be forever.

"yes, I forgive you. I had my own indiscretion, it would be hypocritical for me not to forgive you," I said. But inside I knew something had died. She was my first girlfriend since Stacy and Carole. Maybe I just wasn't meant to have the kind of relationship I wanted. In the recesses of my consciousness I found comfort in not allowing myself to be in love with her, but rather to just be friends and travel partners.

I told her of my travels and the many people I had met like Aad here in Amsterdam, Marcus and Lisa in Lisbon, Ken in Barcelona and the boys in Ibiza. I mentioned how we intended to meet again at the Oktoberfest in Munich. Of course, that was months away, I said and for the time being, we had many countries to explore together. I told her about the car I had purchased and used more money than I wanted but figured we would save on transportation to make up for what I had spent. Christina gave me some more bad news, explaining that she did not bring as much money as she planned because while she was in Seattle her purse was stolen and much of her savings was in her wallet. I realized then that we probably could only last a couple of months on our combined fortunes.

The pain in my chest from Christina's disclosure lasted for a couple of days but I was good at sweeping pain like that away for the time being and I enjoyed showing her what I knew of Amsterdam. We spent more time walking around the city, then went to the Rijksmuseum and of course the Heineken Brewery. The next day was her birthday and we boarded the train to Zandvoort and spent the day at the beach. It was there that we began our summer-long gin rummy tournament of two.

By day three, I was ready to pack up the VW and hit the road. We drove to Germany through Frankfurt and camped outside of Nuremberg. We then drove south to Garmisch, where I showed her the place Jerry and I had spent so much time three years previous. We kept moving and ended up arriving in North Italy where we found a campground outside of Venice. We slept on the ground with only the plastic tube tent as a mattress. Chris was not used to this but because she was young, she adapted quickly as our mission was to save money by sleeping in campgrounds as often as possible.

As would happen, many times over the next couple of months we enjoyed having mini vacations at the many destinations we visited. We met people, some Americans, some characters from other countries that both charmed and annoyed us and because Chris was so friendly, I took a backseat to her ability to make new friends. We stayed three nights in the campground in Vicenza, spending days reading, talking and playing gin rummy. One of the days we drove into Venice to explore that wonderful city and because of our budget were forced to decide on whether to buy a gondola ride through the canals or have dinner at a restaurant. We chose the restaurant. As I look back, I think it would have been nice to take that gondola ride, but I loved dining at an outdoor café as we ate pasta and drank wine, watching the people and boats passing by; so, I probably would still make the same choice today.

On the first day of August, the third day in Vicenza we drove to a beach town that someone had recommended, Jesolo, which was just north of Venice. Our one-day excursion to Jesolo allowed us to discover a charming Seaside village along the Adriatic Sea, where we found a small and inexpensive restaurant and made the decision to splurge and check into a hotel the next night. After camping for five consecutive nights, it was time to feel the comfort of a real bed. So, the following morning, we rolled up our sleeping bags and re-packed my backpack and her carrying case and drove to Jesolo to enjoy the beaches of the Adriatic. We liked it so much we ended up staying two nights in an inexpensive hostel across from the water and beach.

I do not remember the conversations, but I do recall that we were very happy. We were free and independent; without a care other than our money that had to last us if we were to stay another two months. As it turned out, in those two months we would travel to Yugoslavia, Greece, back to Italy, Austria, Switzerland and Germany. I was 25, she had just turned 19 and we became once again, not only lovers but best friends. The contrast from being alone the first three months and now traveling with a companion made the trip not only different but, in many ways richer. Having a friend, that I was growing to love, despite my resolve not to, allowed me to share the experiences. It served as a metaphor for life. Being with someone means compromise and patience, but the reward is companionship. Chris was easy to be with, so it made the journey easy. We quickly fell into a rhythm that allowed us to enjoy what lay ahead. Our days were either traveling or exploring new destinations, camping without a tent at night and when we just could not take it anymore, we would stay in a hotel or hostel. There would be long conversations about life and philosophy, laughter and romantic dinners, with each day a new adventure.

We left Jesolo and Italy, crossing the border to what was then Yugoslavia, a communist country. The country was beautiful, but because of the government repression, the people were different. I remember noticing that the joy I had seen on the faces of the Dutch and the Italians in recent days was missing; in its place, there seemed to be an overall gloom. This country had a brief history, merging three separate countries into one after World War I. Then in World War II, the Nazis invaded this relatively new country and by the end of the war, Communist Russia had dominion as it did the entire Eastern European block of countries. The country at the time we visited was ruled by Josip Tito, who remained in power, until his death in1980. What we did not know at the time was that after Tito's death and the fall of communism in the late 80's, this country would fall into a long and bloody civil war that would eventually lead to breaking it up once again into separate countries.

We slept on the ground in Belgrade, continued to travel south to Skopje and entered one of the darkest storms I had ever seen. Day seemed to turn into night as we watched through the windows of our VW huge black clouds covering up the sun. We knew we needed to find shelter from the apparent storm and stopped at a very odd two-story hotel outside Skopje that seemed to be standing in the middle of nowhere. We were both at the point where sleeping on a bed was a luxury even when the hotel was not first class, especially when during the night we heard the thunder that followed flashes of lighting as the storm sent a torrent of rain down on our residence. When we woke in the morning the sun was out again and we decided we had seen enough of Yugoslavia and made our way south to Greece.

Without knowing where we were going after we crossed the Greek border, we found another beach town, Platamon, on the Aegean Sea. As always, whether it was the Mediterranean, Adriatic or Aegean, the coastal areas were home to us. This one was a different shelter from the storm; not of weather, but from the strange experience of being in a country that appeared not to have a soul.

Once again, we indulged ourselves and stayed two nights at the Hotel Diana near the beach. Then, on the road again to Athens where we arrived sometime in the late evening and slept in the car outside of a campground. I was aware that the boys from South Africa and Canada were planning on being in Greece in August, but we had no plans to meet. I considered how nice it would be to run into them but the chances of that happening were very close to impossible.

We checked into the campground the next morning and looked for one of the vans, but no sight of either anywhere in the campground. The clerk at the campground office said there was another campground in Athens, on the other side of the city. Even though I knew the futility of our search, I was now on a mission. We drove to the other campground and walked into their office. I noticed a large bulletin board with a vast collage of cards and notes pinned to the surface. I looked through the many notes and suddenly one caught my attention. It was a note from Jay to Paul explaining that they had gone to Mykonos and to meet them there. The date was August 9th which was the previous day. Certain that it was my boys, I wrote at the bottom of the note, "Paul, we are in Athens – if you see this, lets meet here at 2 pm, Andy McKay."

Chris and I left to explore Athens and discovered a city crowded, smog filled and dirty, with the most incredible food and of course the ancient ruins of the Acropolis high on a hill that just seemed to sprout up from the somewhat, flat city. We arranged our day so that we would be back at Bill's campground at 2 pm, wondering if he had seen our note. The odds were slim to be sure. I parked the car near the camp office and there he was, waiting for us. Paul was my favorite of the Canadians with his quiet almost shy personality, we had become good friends in Ibiza and Pamplona. He explained that he had lost the key to their van and the rest of the boys left him to find it or get another made while they went on to the island of Mykonos. It was good to see him and as we shook hands, I introduced him to Christina.

I was sorry he had been left alone by the group, it seemed a bit harsh, but I realized that had that not happened we would never have seen him or the others.

We moved our meager camp to Paul's campground and over the course of the next two days the three of us enjoyed discovering Athens. I realized that once we got past the condition of the city, it was actually an interesting place. Athens to me was surprisingly third world for a city that was the birth of civilization, but there was a vibrancy that was almost festive as we walked past outdoor cafes, bars and restaurants. Climbing the hill of the Acropolis we wandered through the Parthenon trying to imagine what it must be like walking through the temple over two thousand years before. The view from the top allowed us to have a 360-degree view of the city below. At the end of the second day with Paul, after a long day of walking and sight-seeing we enjoyed a wonderful Greek dinner sitting outside and immersing ourselves in the culture that was Athens. The only thing that spoiled the two days with Paul was his concern about what to do about the lost car key. We decided to find someone the next day who could make a key.

The next morning, Paul woke with a huge smile as he explained that he found the van key in his bedding. We were now free to follow the boys to Mykonos. We made plans to leave our car and his van at the campground and ferry across from Athens to Mykonos. It was to be another vacation in our travels, and unknown to us, as we cruised the beautiful aqua-blue waters of the Aegean Sea on an overnight ship, another magical ten days.

Chapter 32

WE ARRIVED IN the morning at the sheltered bay of the Mykonos town, called Chora, and were struck by the quaint beauty of the stark white stucco buildings with blue umbrellas and awnings along the bay front shops and restaurants. The cobbled streets were narrow walkways and the houses, the same white but with blue doors and shutters and adorned with colorful Bougainvillea vines. This was indeed a paradise. Behind the shops and houses there was a hill with old fashioned windmills that appeared to be from the period of Don Quixote.

The three of us disembarked the Ferry and found an outdoor café just a few yards from the landing. We had no idea where to go and besides wanting to eat, we needed to get our bearings. One of the waiters in the restaurant spoke English and pointed to a road weaving along the water's edge and explained that there was a restaurant on the south side of the island that allowed young people to sleep on the beach. He said it was about 6 kilometers away. So, after eating and walking up and around the quant little village that could have been a movie set for *Zorba the Greek*, we began the walk to the south side.

The road that led us away from town was only one lane; so narrow that as taxis and occasional buses passed by, we were forced to get out of the way. At the crest of the hill, the view of the Aegean below us was breathtaking; probably the bluest water I had ever seen. It is worth noting that the Mediterranean Sea is the huge body of water that is almost completely enclosed by land, on the north by Southern Europe and Turkey, on the south by North Africa, and the east by Syria, Lebanon and Israel. Within the Mediterranean are smaller bodies of water; bays that are surrounded by land that are also called seas. The Adriatic lies between Italy's eastern edge and what used to be Yugoslavia. The Aegean Sea is between Greece and Turkey and is part of many of the Greek islands. The Ionian Sea is bounded by Southern Italy and Western Greece and Albania. It is really all Mediterranean Sea and its shores are some of the most interesting lands of the world.

As we walked, the three of us were absolutely giddy with joy over this new-found paradise. We finally came upon the beach at the end of the road and if there was anything beyond this point, we never saw it. It appeared that the road just abruptly ended. What we did see were tents and sleeping bags on an empty lot just behind the restaurant. We found a table inside the restaurant, put our gear down on the ground by our chairs and ordered beers. As were all the buildings on the island, this restaurant was white stucco, with blue trim and open air, with only a half wall separating the restaurant from the beach, offering, of course, an amazing view of the water. What we had been told in town was true, we could sleep on the lot or on the beach, use the restaurant bathroom and stay at the tables as long as we wanted, playing cards, checkers or backgammon. It was hot, especially after our walk and soon we were in our swimsuits walking to the beach and diving into the refreshing water that was about the temperature of most swimming pools in the summer. This was the beginning of our holiday on the Island of Mykonos.

Today, as I write this, I would easily pay thousands of dollars for the experience we had for just the cost of food and beer each day. It did not take long before we had established our routine. The first night Chris and I slept on the beach but discovered it was not as comfortable as the hard ground behind the restaurant. When we woke each morning as the sun was rising over the hill behind us, we would dive into the sea for a wakeup; then have coffee and bread with butter and honey for breakfast. Chris wrote postcards, I read or played cards with Ken, then we swam some more before hosing off the saltwater from a water hose behind the restaurant. Freshly clean and dressed we would walk to Chora for the evening.

We knew that the rest of the boys were somewhere on the island but did not spend a lot of time thinking about it. We were quite content with our current situation. It was on the third night, however, that the three of us bumped into Michael in town and he led us to a restaurant where Trevor, Jay and Brian were having beers. I introduced everyone to Christina, and we got caught up on what they were doing since they got to Mykonos. It seemed they had found a place that was about a mile over the hill on the other side of the island called Paradise Beach. They explained that there, it was clothing optional. We agreed to go see them the next day.

When we arrived after our usual swim and breakfast on our own beach, we discovered a very strange cultural phenomenon. There was a mass of young people about our age that seemed sort of drugged out; perhaps they were. I never saw drugs but the people, even our friends were kind of in this trance like space, most of them completely naked. I told Chris I was not comfortable, and she agreed. It was too weird. We stayed long enough to be polite, had a couple of beers, swam but did not take our clothes off. Before we left, Paul announced he wanted to get his gear from our camp and join the boys. Trevor, on the other hand, wanted out of Paradise Beach and came with us. Trevor and I had already forged a strong friendship while in Ibiza and Pamplona and that friendship became even stronger over the next few days with the three of us hanging out at our little beach.

Trevor loved the lifestyle we had created during the day, playing cards and board games, talking philosophy and the politics of both South Africa and America while eating bread and French fries then swimming and taking naps on the beach as our skin became golden brown. Since there was no night life at our little retreat, we would after cleaning up, go into town for fabulous Greek food. My favorite became Souvlaki; shaved lamb meat on a Pita sandwich with that wonderful cucumber sauce called Tzatziki. At dusk, the little village came alive with locals and tourists wandering from bar to restaurant that were decorated with twinkling lights that created a magical ambiance. On one of the nights there was an outdoor movie right in the middle of the square. Chairs were placed in rows in the courtyard and a screen was set up that was like an enlarged old home movie screen. I'm not sure where the projector was placed, it was a detail that did not interest me, but the movie was not that old, and it was fun drinking beer and eating Souvlaki while watching the show. This was certainly a time in our lives where we had not a care in the world; a dream come true. But like all dreams, it was eventually over and time for us to return to Athens and our next destination.

Chris and I stayed in Athens for three more days then said goodbye to the boys, again promising to meet in Munich, and drove north-west to catch a ferry to the island of Corfu. Our intention was to take another ferry from there to Italy to avoid going back through Yugoslavia. We found a hostel on the island and enjoyed just being the two of us again. We did not really do much, just drove around the perimeter and explored the beaches. On one of the days we had a picnic on a beautiful lush lawn while watching a Cricket Match that we did not understand at all. Corfu is one of the larger islands that are part of several located along the Ionian Sea. While Mykonos is mostly baron, almost like a desert, Corfu has a climate that is ideal for forests and Olive Trees. The English influence comes from the fact that it was owned by the English before they gave it to Greece in 1864.

Sometime during our stay in Corfu, we discovered that the cost of taking the ferry with our car across to Italy was more than we wanted to spend and so made the decision to go back through Yugoslavia to get to Italy. After four relaxing days in Corfu, we headed back to Athens for one night where we took in the Daphne Wine Festival and drank some of the worst wine I ever tasted.

Chapter 33

IT WAS NOW September and we had several places to see before going to the Oktoberfest at the end of the month. We went back to Platamon Beach where we camped for one night before crossing over to Yugoslavia again and up to Belgrade, Sarajevo and Rijeka over a three-day period, camping each night. One night it rained, and we slept in the car; enduring a tough night in our cramped VW. During this part of our travels, we were not aware of what was going on in the rest of the world and had no knowledge of two critical events happening this first week of September. In Munich where we planned to meet the boys, the Olympics were taking place. About the time that we were traveling once again through Yugoslavia 8 members of a terrorist group called Black September entered the Olympic Village and knocked at the door of the room where the Israeli athletes were staying. In the following 24 hours, hostage negotiations were taking place as the terrorists demanded the release of 234 Palestinian prisoners in Israel. The result of the ensuing developments was that all 11 athletes were murdered as well as all but 3 terrorists, who escaped but were later captured. It was this International event that brought light to terrorism in the world.

The other event that was occurring during the summer was the discovery of a burglary in the Democratic Headquarters at the Watergate Complex in Washington D.C. This of course was the beginning of the end of Richard Nixon's Presidency. Even though he was elected in November of that year, he would not survive the scandal and would resign two years later.

As all this was happening, we drove back to Italy where we camped once gain near Venice. We continued south to Florence and then Rome where we found an inexpensive bungalow while we visited that stunning city.

Driving in Rome was like driving in Paris, maybe even worse because those Italians were aggressive and crazy behind the wheel. We decided to just keep the car parked while we explored the city. My memories of the visit are blurred but I recall sitting on the Spanish

Steps along with other tourists from all over the world. I remember the Tivoli Fountain and Christina and I throwing coins in while making a wish. The most impressive of all the history that Rome had to offer was the Vatican and the Sistine Chapel. After seeing the sculptor of David in Florence and the masterpiece painted on the ceiling of the Sistine Chapel, I had an appreciation of the genius of Michael Angelo and his art. One of the very few souvenirs of the trip was a book I purchased of the works of Michelangelo, which I still have.

Within the first two weeks of September we had visited both Rome and Athens, the two early civilizations that shaped both government and philosophy. Our travels brought us to appreciate art, architecture and cultures but as mentioned before, for me the most interesting part of the travel were the people; both the ones we met and those we observed, which is no different now than it was then. They are rich or poor, happy or angry, funny or sad, but most are just somewhere in the middle just trying to do the best they can to carve out a meaningful existence. Over the course of our travels, we met some very interesting people most of whom I cannot remember but nevertheless made impressions on our young and curious minds.

On the 15ᵗʰ of September we left Rome and drove North to Switzerland. Our trip was almost over. As we drove through the heavy forest area between Zurich and Interlaken, we saw a familiar gray van with the mouse that said Boerie Tours parked on the side of the road. It was the Canadians who now was with a South African I had not met, Richard Stoffberg who I would later call Joe Cool because he was. Rich, as he was called, was very handsome with dark curly hair and the brilliant blue eyes and a smile that said, I am in control. Chris and I liked him immediately as we talked to the boys about where they had been recently and where they were going. There seemed to be a network of other South Africans, traveling like our friends and most knew each other since they were all from Durban. That is how the Canadiens met Casper, who was traveling alone when they all were in the same campground somewhere in Italy after leaving Greece. They were now headed for Interlaken and we decided to follow them.

It was beginning to get cold at night both from the change in seasons and the fact we were surrounded by mountains. We stayed in Interlaken for three nights and ended up sleeping in the van because of the rain and cold. We loved Interlaken an absolutely, gorgeous area and quaint little city where we strolled along charming streets looking at shops and stopping to have a hot chocolate as we enjoyed this weather change. Sleeping in the van, however, was not comfortable since we only had space between the front seat and the bed behind, maybe 3 feet, allowing us only to sleep on our sides. By the end of the three nights our bodies ached to be in a real bed again.

We left the boys and Switzerland, driving over the Alps to Garmisch-Partenkirchen where we secured a room for two nights. While we were there, we climbed up mountain trails marveling at the rolling green hills below and the sheer beauty of this area. While hiking we met a young couple on their honeymoon, Peter and Pat, and enjoyed just sitting at a rest area high in the mountain getting to hear their story as we told them ours.

By the time we left Garmisch, we were nearly out of money. It was time for the Oktoberfest, which takes place during the last week of September, so we drove to Munich to meet our friends at a predetermined time and place. As I would discover, the Oktoberfest was very much like the Hofbrau House that I had visited with Jerry, Mac and Stephanie three years before, but is expanded twenty times. It was a massive carnival like atmosphere much like a county fair with tents set up to serve as beer halls. For our group, it was just one big wonderful party, marking for many of us, the end of our travels. For the locals, it must have been a profound contrast after just experiencing the Olympics and the murder of those Israeli athletes.

Chris and I put the word out to our group that we wanted to sell our car. I had purchased it for $300 but was asking $200 which we needed to finish our trip. At this point we had no idea when we would be going home; a lot depended on our money. As it turned out, on the second day of the festival a female friend of the South Africans, who had just arrived in Europe offered us $150 and we decided to take it. So now we had no car, but we had money and we celebrated by getting a room.

The following day Chris and I walked around Munich and saw a travel agency, which was always easy to spot because of the colorful travel pictures displayed on the business windows. We went in to check flight schedules; deciding we needed to plan our departure. My original intention was to stay 6 months, thinking at the time that the Oktoberfest was in October, not September. The plan was to leave after the festival, but I was determined to not leave before October, so we booked our return home for October 5th, which would be for me 5 months and 5 days in Europe. We now had 8 days left and no plans on how we would finish or what we would do. Of course, we really didn't plan too much of the trip and that loose itinerary is what made it so much more interesting. To this day, I find tours and over planning of vacations boring and for the most part, this has how I have lived my life, which probably has lent to mistakes and even failures, but has created a very interesting life journey.

We ended up staying in our room two nights then went with the boys to a campground where they were staying on the edge of Munich. The day we moved was also the day that Michael left for Durban. We all saw him off at the Munich train station that was to take him eventually to London for his return flight back to South Africa. The days were getting colder now, and the change of the seasons and the departure of Michael left a growing sadness for the end of our trip as well. It would be another six years before we would see Michael again. We had become very fond of him; a somewhat careful and conservative young man who could be the life of the party and somewhat rowdy with a few beers in him. He kept up his persona by getting well intoxicated before boarding the train.

On our last night in Munich as the festival was ending, we ran into another character from Sheffield, England; Rob McCarthy. He had short cropped hair, dark horn-rimmed oval glasses and a dark mustache. We befriended him and stayed in touch, eventually seeing him in California the following winter.

We left Munich on the last day of September with the Canadians who agreed to transport us to Amsterdam. We said our goodbyes to Trevor and Clive, both would eventually immigrate to the U.S and remain life-long friends. Still, we had no way of knowing that at the time and it was once again hard to say goodbye when you realized we might never meet again.

Since we had 5 days left, we decided to drive to Berlin. It was now too cold to sleep outside so Chris and I spent the next 3 nights once again sleeping in that space between the front seat and the back bed. Even for as young as we were, sleeping on one side without being able to turn around was not pleasant. We were, however, grateful to have the transportation and a place to keep warm.

Berlin was our last city to visit before returning to Amsterdam. We parked the van on the west side of the city and decided to cross over on foot at Checkpoint Charlie to East Berlin. It was a very strange experience seeing the famous wall that was designed to keep people imprisoned in the communist side of the city. It was obvious as we walked into the East side why communism did not work and why people wanted out. The contrast between the two sides was quite startling. West Berlin, now 25 years past the end of World War II was a modern and vibrant city, with no remnants of that war that left rubble in much of the city. On the east side the buildings that had been re-built, were gray and cold with nothing exciting architecturally. Like our drive through Yugoslavia, East Berlin had a very repressed vibe that we felt immediately. We walked around for a couple of miles but were quite pleased to be able to return to the other side. The history of that wall and the repression of the Soviet Countries is indeed a very sad chapter of how the spoils of World War II were divided and how those people that were left on the Soviet side continued to suffer for another generation after that war.

We left Berlin and headed toward Amsterdam spending one more night sleeping in the Van on the side of the road. It was Tuesday September 3rd when we rolled into the city that had been the gateway of both of my European adventures. The Canadians were not going to stay in Amsterdam but move on to London there point of departure. Once again it was time to say goodbye. They were brothers, gracious to take us along and would be friends for many years in the future. Jay and Paul would visit us in Fresno the first year after we met, and we would see them all again in 1976 when we drove from Fresno to Richmond, British Columbia.

Now we had just enough money to rent an inexpensive room for our last two nights. The first of those we went to a movie. The following day our last, we strolled the streets, along the canals that I had first introduced to Chris two months earlier. We made plans to have our own Farwell-party by going to a nice restaurant. On that last day we ran into Rob McCarthy, who joined us for drinks in one of the many lounges before dinner. While we drank, we met a couple, Steve and Riki, who had just arrived from the U.S. and we all had lively discussions about life, travel and what was going to be next. I found it strange that once again, as in 1969, to meet new arrivals while planning our departure.

The next morning, we had one last walk around the section of the City that I loved so much. Little did I know that I would not be back again for many years as we boarded a bus to Schiphol Airport. We boarded a Lufthansa jumbo jet that was to take us to Chicago and then on to Los Angeles. After 5 months, I was looking forward to going home. I found some earphones on my seat and plugged in to the music that was provided. For the first time, I heard a new song by Led Zeppelin, *Stairway to Heaven*. As I listened to the words, I thought what an appropriate song to hear as we taxied down the runway, the last leg of a journey I had spent a year planning and saving to create.

During those months and years since Europe, 1969 my dream was to return. This trip in 1972 was the result of an intention that became an obsession, a resolve that would not be deterred. Now it was over and though I did not know it at the time, ideas that came to me over my lifetime I would continue to pursue. Some would work, some did not, but I had established a pattern

Now, we both wondered what would be next? Where would our lives take us, what new adventures were ahead? I was 25, Chris was 19 and as the Carpenters Song said, we had only just begun.

Epilogue

I DO NOT believe in "Happily Ever After". The concept of happily ever after, seems boring to me. Life is a journey; a great adventure that offers challenges and opportunities; sometimes cloaked in the same garment. Overcoming challenges allows us to grow and expand our soul. For me, it is always wondering, what is next? If we know it will be the same year after year, is that happily ever after? For some, I suppose it is, but not for me. Perhaps it was the experiences of those early years; maybe it is just who I am at my Core.

Christina and I were married in June of 1973, nine months after our return from Europe. Tom Spencer was my best man and Clive and Trevor, who had moved to California from South Africa were at our reception as was Jay and another Canadian friend of his. It was not long after we returned to the US, that we received a letter from Trevor, explaining that the South African girl who bought our VW in Munich had driven to the Dutch Border, where the car was originally registered, and it was impounded. Apparently, our little blue VW Beetle was a stolen car. We felt terrible that the poor girl had given up $150 for the short ride from Munich to Holland. I realized what those guys in Paris were up to, selling stolen cars. We were lucky; we had driven all over the continent of Europe for two months in a stolen car without a clue.

Trevor had two friends in Durban that had traveled in Europe the year before us who had met a young American, whose father was connected to the City College in San Diego and sponsored the three of them to come to the U.S. to attend that college. All three immigrants obtained their citizenship and thrived individually. Clive also moved to the U.S. soon after the end of the European trip and Michael followed six years later. Both also obtained citizenship. I often wondered if that would ever have happened if they had not had the adventure in their souls to make the trip to Europe in the first place.

We learned that Richard Stoffburg, (Joe Cool), died young from Cancer. The Canadians remained in Richmond, British Columbia and all three came down to see us in the first couple of years after 1972. In 1976, after I finally graduated from Cal State Fresno, Chris and I bought a Porsche 914 and drove up the coast to Canada to see the boys. A few years after, we learned that Jay had passed away.

We spent Christmas in 1978 in South Africa, traveling with Trevor and his wife and met Trev's family in Durban. Chris and I stayed with Clive's parents for the week we were there, allowing us to immerse ourselves in the culture of Apartheid South Africa. There would be many changes in the years to come that would change the country, but then, that is another story.

Over the years, I somehow got caught up chasing money and success, which was what I had cautioned myself against on my birthday in Pamplona. Along the way I lost myself in the process. Chris and I had a good life in those early years, and I was considered a success at an early age, buying and selling real estate. Unfortunately, it did not last. I made many bad decisions in my business adventures that sabotaged any success and accumulation of money I planned to accomplish in my life. Still, as mentioned, challenges bring opportunity. The wheels came off my real estate fix and flip business but took me in a career direction that became my life's work. I obtained my real estate license in 1976 and sold for several years. In 1980, the market took a dive due to huge inflation and we lost the bulk of our properties, but I was still able to make a good living selling.

In 1987 we moved to Newport Beach, where I began working with my best friend Tom on development projects. The partnership worked for a short time and of course Chris and I enjoyed living in the paradise that is Newport. Once again, the market took another dive, this time due to a Savings and Loan crisis that brought many companies down with it. Eventually Tom and I separated our partnership and the result strained our friendship for a few years. It was a very difficult time for me as I had to find work to support an expensive lifestyle, eventually getting into the real estate training and seminar business; and even though Newport was a paradise, the people I encountered were not so nice. I discovered that business in that arena was hard core tough and I just was not able to compete. I had to look at my self deeply to see what I wanted to do career wise and realized, I was good at sales and good with people. My career path took another turn as we moved back to Fresno and I took a job as a sales manager for a large real estate company.

During those years of success and failure our children were born, and it was that part of our life that was best during our stormy financial years. We had two girls, Teresa and Grace that have been the light of both our lives throughout the many years since they were born. But the last business failure in Newport left a residue as some of the people I worked with in the speaking business filed lawsuits against me. Even while I was climbing back up the ladder of success as a sales manager, I realized not only had I lost my joy, I really was broken; functionally broken, no one knew but eventually the soul that I lost somewhere, led me to leave Christina after 22 years of being together.

I set myself adrift on other adventures, changing companies, starting my own company and chasing love. I know there are many who have regrets for roads not traveled. While I have regrets, most of them were from choosing a different road and discovering it was not what I wanted. There are very few roads my soul or ego did not take, but the challenge for someone like me was choosing whether it was my soul or my ego that chose the road. Too often is was the ego.

I have often wondered that if success is important, then how do you measure it? I truly believe the object of life is to find our true self in the chaos that lures us into reaching for the so called "brass ring." My true soul self, as I have learned, has not been in building a fortune, but rather in service both in my profession and in the community. On my journey, I discovered that true happiness comes from the freedom to be and enjoy the person that God intended us to be. We are not what we do, we are who we become when we allow ourselves the freedom to be the person we were meant to be. The saying of the decades of my search for success was, "he who dies with the most toys, wins." I know now that statement is and have changed it to say, "he who dies with the most joy, wins." Happily ever after, can only be achieved when you bring happiness to everything you do as I told Marcus in Lisbon on a hot summer day that summer of 1972.

Now, as I enter a whole new frontier, my 70's, I find a relaxed acceptance of the wonderful journey that has been my life. I am happy to say that although there have been mistakes, for the most part I have had a fantastic adventure and still believe, I will never grow old. It is understanding, as long as I get to be on this planet, I can create another exhilarating chapter by bringing happiness, freedom and God along the journey. So far it has been a hell of a ride and now, once again, I find myself wondering, what's next?

Printed in the United States
By Bookmasters